# Get Ready!

## FOR STANDARDIZED TESTS

GRADE FIVE 5

**Other Books in the *Get Ready!* Series:**

*Get Ready! for Standardized Tests: Grade 1* by Joseph Harris, Ph.D.

*Get Ready! for Standardized Tests: Grade 2* by Joseph Harris, Ph.D.

*Get Ready! for Standardized Tests: Grade 3* by Karen Mersky, Ph.D.

*Get Ready! for Standardized Tests: Grade 4* by Joseph Harris, Ph.D.

*Get Ready! for Standardized Tests: Grade 6* by Shirley Vickery, Ph.D.

# Get Ready!

## FOR STANDARDIZED TESTS

### GRADE FIVE

Leslie E. Talbott, Ph.D.

Carol Turkington
Series Editor

**McGraw-Hill**

New York    San Francisco    Washington, D.C.    Auckland    Bogotá
Caracas    Lisbon    London    Madrid    Mexico City    Milan
Montreal    New Delhi    San Juan    Singapore
Sydney    Tokyo    Toronto

**Library of Congress Cataloging-in-Publication Data**

Get ready! for standardized tests / c Carol Turkington, series editor.
      p. cm.
   Includes bibliographical references.
   Contents: [1] Grade 1 / Joseph Harris — [2] Grade 2 / Joseph Harris — [3] Grade 3 /
Karen Mersky — [4] Grade 4 / Joseph Harris — [5] Grade 5 / Leslie E. Talbott — [6]
Grade 6 / Shirley Vickery.
   ISBN 0-07-136010-7 (v. 1) — ISBN 0-07-136011-5 (v. 2) — ISBN 0-07-136012-3 (v. 3)
— ISBN 0-07-136013-1 (v. 4) — ISBN 0-07-136014-X (v. 5) — ISBN 0-07-136015-8 (v. 6)
   1. Achievement tests—United States—Study guides.  2. Education, Elementary—United
States—Evaluation.  3. Education, Elementary—Parent participation—United States.  I.
Turkington, Carol.  II. Harris, Joseph.

LB3060.22 .G48   2000
372.126—dc21                            00-056083

*McGraw-Hill*

*A Division of The **McGraw·Hill** Companies*

  2 3 4 5 6 7 8 9 0 PBT/PBT 0 9 8 7 6 5 4 3 2 1 0

ISBN 0-07-136014-X

*This book was set in New Century Schoolbook by Inkwell Publishing Services.*

*Printed and bound by Phoenix Book Technology.*

To my sons Bill and Daniel Raskind,
whose lives were the best books I ever read about learning.
And to my mother, Kay Williams Talbott,
whose example was the best book I ever read on parenting.

# Contents

**Skills Checklist**     **xi**

**Introduction**     **1**
Types of Standardized Tests     1
The Major Standardized Tests     2
How States Use Standardized Tests     2
Valid Uses of Standardized Test Scores     3
Inappropriate Use of Standardized
    Test Scores     3
Two Basic Assumptions     4
A Word about Coaching     4
How to Raise Test Scores     4
Test Questions     5

**Chapter 1. Test-Taking Basics**     **7**
The Fifth Grader's Development     7
Test-Taking Skills Your Child Needs     8
How You Can Help Your Child     11

**Chapter 2. Vocabulary**     **15**
What You and Your Child Can Do     15
What Tests May Ask     16
Basic Vocabulary     16
    What Your Fifth Grader Should Be
       Learning     17
    What You Can Do     17
    Practice Skills: Basic Vocabulary     17
Synonyms and Antonyms     17
    What Your Fifth Grader Should Be
       Learning     18

What You Can Do     18
Practice Skills: Synonyms     18
Practice Skills: Antonyms     18
Multi-Meaning Words     19
    What Your Fifth Grader Should Be
       Learning     19
    What You Can Do     19
    Practice Skills: Multi-Meaning Words     19
Words in Context     20
    What Your Fifth Grader Should Be
       Learning     20
    What You Can Do     20
    Practice Skills: Words in Context     20
Word Study     21
    What Your Fifth Grader Should Be
       Learning     21
    What You Can Do     21
    Prefixes and Suffixes     21
    Practice Skills: Word Study     22

**Chapter 3. Reading
Comprehension**     **23**
Goals for Fifth Graders     23
What You and Your Child Can Do     23
What Tests May Ask     24
Literal Comprehension     24
    What Your Fifth Grader Should Be
       Learning     24
    What You Can Do     24
    What Tests May Ask     24
    Practice Skills: Literal Comprehension     24

Critical Reading and Inferential
  Comprehension  25
What Your Fifth Grader Should Be
  Learning  25
What You Can Do  25
What Tests May Ask  26
Practice Skills: Inferential
  Comprehension and Critical Reading  26

## Chapter 4. Language Mechanics  29

Education Goals for Fifth Graders  29
What You and Your Child Can Do  29
Capitalization  30
What Your Fifth Grader Should Be
  Learning  30
What You Can Do  30
Punctuation  30
What Your Fifth Grader Should Be
  Learning  31
What You Can Do  31
Practice Skills: Capitalization and
  Punctuation  31

## Chapter 5. Language Expression  33

Education Goals for Fifth Graders  33
What You and Your Child Can Do  33
What Tests May Ask  33
Parts of Speech  33
What Your Fifth Grader Should Be
  Learning  34
What You Can Do  34
Practice Skills: Parts of Speech  35
Correct Usage  36
What Your Fifth Grader Should Be
  Learning  36
What You Can Do  36
Practice Skills: Correct Usage  36
Topic Sentences  37
What Your Fifth Grader Should Be
  Learning  37
What You Can Do  37
What Tests May Ask  37
Practice Skills: Topic Sentences  38

## Chapter 6. Spelling and Study Skills  39

Education Goals for Fifth Graders  39
What Tests May Ask  39
Spelling  39
What Your Fifth Grader Should Be
  Learning  39
What You Can Do  39
Practice Skills: Spelling  41
Study Skills  41
What Your Fifth Grader Should Be
  Learning  41
What You Can Do  42
Practice Skills: Study Skills  42

## Chapter 7. Math Concepts  45

Education Goals for Fifth Graders  45
What You and Your Child Can Do  45
What Tests May Ask  46
Numeration  46
What Your Fifth Grader Should Be
  Learning  46
What You Can Do  47
Practice Skills: Numeration  48
Number Concepts  49
What Your Fifth Grader Should Be
  Learning  49
What You Can Do  49
Roman Numerals  50
Place Value  50
Number Patterns  50
Practice Skills: Number Concepts  51
Number Properties  52
What Your Fifth Grader Should Be
  Learning  52
What You Can Do  52
Practice Skills: Number Properties  52
Fractions and Decimals  53
What Your Fifth Grader Should Be
  Learning  53
What You Can Do  53
Practice Skills: Decimals and
  Fractions  54

## Chapter 8. Math Computation — 57

Education Goals for Fifth Graders — 57
What You and Your Child Can Do — 57
What Tests May Ask — 57
Regrouping — 58
Long and Short Division — 58
Fractions — 58
Practice Skills: Math Computation — 59

## Chapter 9. Math Applications — 63

Education Goals for Fifth Graders — 63
What You and Your Child Can Do — 63
What Tests May Ask — 63
Geometry — 64
What Your Fifth Grader Should Be Learning — 64
What You Can Do — 64
Practice Skills: Geometry — 64
Measurement — 66
What Your Fifth Grader Should Be Learning — 66
What You Can Do — 66
Temperature — 66
Money Skills — 67
Elapsed Time — 67
Practice Skills: Measurement — 67
Problem Solving — 69
What Your Fifth Grader Should Be Learning — 69
What You Can Do — 69
Practice Skills: Problem Solving — 70

## Appendix A: Web Sites and Resources for More Information — 73

## Appendix B: Read More about It — 77

## Appendix C: What Your Child's Test Scores Mean — 79

## Appendix D: Which States Require Which Tests — 87

## Appendix E: Testing Accommodations — 97

## Glossary — 99

## Answer Keys for Practice Skills — 101

## Sample Practice Test — 103

## Answer Key for Sample Practice Test — 127

# SKILLS CHECKLIST

| MY CHILD ... | HAS LEARNED | IS WORKING ON |
|---|---|---|
| **VOCABULARY** | | |
| Basic vocabulary | | |
| Synonyms | | |
| Antonyms | | |
| Multi-meaning words | | |
| Words in context | | |
| Word study | | |
| **READING COMPREHENSION** | | |
| Literal comprehension | | |
| Critical reading | | |
| Inferential comprehension | | |
| **LANGUAGE MECHANICS** | | |
| Capitalization | | |
| Punctuation | | |
| **LANGUAGE EXPRESSION** | | |
| Parts of speech | | |
| Correct usage | | |
| Topic sentences | | |
| **SPELLING AND STUDY SKILLS** | | |
| Spelling | | |
| Study skills | | |
| **MATH CONCEPTS** | | |
| Numeration | | |
| Number concepts | | |
| Number properties | | |
| Fractions | | |
| Decimals | | |
| **MATH COMPUTATION** | | |
| Regrouping | | |
| Long division | | |
| Short division | | |
| Fractions | | |
| **MATH APPLICATIONS** | | |
| Geometry | | |
| Measurement | | |
| Problem solving | | |

# Introduction

Almost all of us have taken standardized tests in school. We spent several days bubbling-in answers, shifting in our seats. No one ever told us why we took the tests or what they would do with the results. We just took them and never heard about them again.

Today many parents aren't aware they are entitled to see their children's permanent records and, at a reasonable cost, to obtain copies of any information not protected by copyright, including testing scores. Late in the school year, most parents receive standardized test results with confusing bar charts and detailed explanations of scores that few people seem to understand.

In response to a series of negative reports on the state of education in this country, Americans have begun to demand that something be done to improve our schools. We have come to expect higher levels of accountability as schools face the competing pressures of rising educational expectations and declining school budgets. High-stakes standardized tests are rapidly becoming the main tool of accountability for students, teachers, and school administrators. If students' test scores don't continually rise, teachers and principals face the potential loss of school funding and, ultimately, their jobs. Summer school and private after-school tutorial program enrollments are swelling with students who have not met score standards or who, everyone agrees, could score higher.

While there is a great deal of controversy about whether it is appropriate for schools to use standardized tests to make major decisions about individual students, it appears likely that standardized tests are here to stay. They will be used to evaluate students, teachers, and the schools; schools are sure to continue to use students' test scores to demonstrate their accountability to the community.

The purposes of this guide are to acquaint you with the types of standardized tests your children may take; to help you understand the test results; and to help you work with your children in skill areas that are measured by standardized tests so they can perform as well as possible.

## Types of Standardized Tests

The two major types of group standardized tests are *criterion-referenced tests* and *norm-referenced tests*. Think back to when you learned to tie your shoes. First Mom or Dad showed you how to loosen the laces on your shoe so that you could insert your foot; then they showed you how to tighten the laces—but not too tight. They showed you how to make bows and how to tie a knot. All the steps we just described constitute what is called a *skills hierarchy:* a list of skills from easiest to most difficult that are related to some goal, such as tying a shoelace.

Criterion-referenced tests are designed to determine at what level students are performing on various skills hierarchies. These tests assume that development of skills follows a sequence of steps. For example, if you were teaching shoelace tying, the skills hierarchy might appear this way:

1. Loosen laces.

2. Insert foot.

3. Tighten laces.

4. Make loops with both lace ends.

5. Tie a square knot.

Criterion-referenced tests try to identify how far along the skills hierarchy the student has progressed. There is no comparison against anyone else's score, only against an expected skill level. The main question criterion-referenced tests ask is: "Where is this child in the development of this group of skills?"

Norm-referenced tests, in contrast, are typically constructed to compare children in their abilities as to different skills areas. Although the experts who design test items may be aware of skills hierarchies, they are more concerned with how much of some skill the child has mastered, rather than at what level on the skills hierarchy the child is.

Ideally, the questions on these tests range from very easy items to those that are impossibly difficult. The essential feature of norm-referenced tests is that scores on these measures can be compared to scores of children in similar groups. They answer this question: "How does the child compare with other children of the same age or grade placement in the development of this skill?"

This book provides strategies for increasing your child's scores on both standardized norm-referenced and criterion-referenced tests.

## The Major Standardized Tests

Many criterion-referenced tests currently in use are created locally or (at best) on a state level,

and there are far too many of them to go into detail here about specific tests. However, children prepare for them in basically the same way they do for norm-referenced tests.

A very small pool of norm-referenced tests is used throughout the country, consisting primarily of the Big Five:

- California Achievement Tests (CTB/McGraw-Hill)

- Iowa Tests of Basic Skills (Riverside)

- Metropolitan Achievement Test (Harcourt-Brace & Company)

- Stanford Achievement Test (Psychological Corporation)

- TerraNova [formerly Comprehensive Test of Basic Skills] (McGraw-Hill)

These tests use various terms for the academic skills areas they assess, but they generally test several types of reading, language, and mathematics skills, along with social studies and science. They may include additional assessments, such as of study and reference skills.

## How States Use Standardized Tests

Despite widespread belief and practice to the contrary, group standardized tests are designed to assess and compare the achievement of groups. They are *not* designed to provide detailed diagnostic assessments of individual students. (For detailed individual assessments, children should be given individual diagnostic tests by properly qualified professionals, including trained guidance counselors, speech and language therapists, and school psychologists.) Here are examples of the types of questions group standardized tests are designed to answer:

- How did the reading achievement of students at Valley Elementary School this year compare with their reading achievement last year?

- How did math scores at Wonderland Middle School compare with those of students at Parkside Middle School this year?

- As a group, how did Hilltop High School students compare with the national averages in the achievement areas tested?

- How did the district's first graders' math scores compare with the district's fifth graders' math scores?

The fact that these tests are designed primarily to test and compare groups doesn't mean that test data on individual students isn't useful. It does mean that when we use these tests to diagnose individual students, we are using them for a purpose for which they were not designed.

Think of group standardized tests as being similar to health fairs at the local mall. Rather than check into your local hospital and spend thousands of dollars on full, individual tests for a wide range of conditions, you can go from station to station and take part in different health screenings. Of course, one would never diagnose heart disease or cancer on the basis of the screening done at the mall. At most, suspicious results on the screening would suggest that you need to visit a doctor for a more complete examination.

In the same way, group standardized tests provide a way of screening the achievement of many students quickly. Although you shouldn't diagnose learning problems solely based on the results of these tests, the results can tell you that you should think about referring a child for a more definitive, individual assessment.

An individual student's group test data should be considered only a point of information. Teachers and school administrators may use standardized test results to support or question hypotheses they have made about students; but these scores must be used alongside other information, such as teacher comments, daily work, homework, class test grades, parent observations, medical needs, and social history.

## Valid Uses of Standardized Test Scores

Here are examples of appropriate uses of test scores for individual students:

- Mr. Cone thinks that Samantha, a third grader, is struggling in math. He reviews her file and finds that her first- and second-grade standardized test math scores were very low. Her first- and second-grade teachers recall episodes in which Samantha cried because she couldn't understand certain math concepts, and mention that she was teased by other children, who called her "Dummy." Mr. Cone decides to refer Samantha to the school assistance team to determine whether she should be referred for individual testing for a learning disability related to math.

- The local college wants to set up a tutoring program for elementary school children who are struggling academically. In deciding which youngsters to nominate for the program, the teachers consider the students' averages in different subjects, the degree to which students seem to be struggling, parents' reports, and standardized test scores.

- For the second year in a row, Gene has performed poorly on the latest round of standardized tests. His teachers all agree that Gene seems to have some serious learning problems. They had hoped that Gene was immature for his class and that he would do better this year; but his dismal grades continue. Gene is referred to the school assistance team to determine whether he should be sent to the school psychologist for assessment of a possible learning handicap.

## Inappropriate Use of Standardized Test Scores

Here are examples of how schools have sometimes used standardized test results inappropriately:

- Mr. Johnson groups his students into reading groups solely on the basis of their standardized test scores.

- Ms. Henry recommends that Susie be held back a year because she performed poorly on the standardized tests, despite strong grades on daily assignments, homework, and class tests.

- Gerald's teacher refers him for consideration in the district's gifted program, which accepts students using a combination of intelligence test scores, achievement test scores, and teacher recommendations. Gerald's intelligence test scores were very high. Unfortunately, he had a bad cold during the week of the standardized group achievement tests and was taking powerful antihistamines, which made him feel sleepy. As a result, he scored too low on the achievement tests to qualify.

The public has come to demand increasingly high levels of accountability for public schools. We demand that schools test so that we have hard data with which to hold the schools accountable. But too often, politicians and the public place more faith in the test results than is justified. Regardless of whether it's appropriate to do so and regardless of the reasons schools use standardized test results as they do, many schools base crucial programming and eligibility decisions on scores from group standardized tests. It's to your child's advantage, then, to perform as well as possible on these tests.

## Two Basic Assumptions

The strategies we present in this book come from two basic assumptions:

1. Most students can raise their standardized test scores.

2. Parents can help their children become stronger in the skills the tests assess.

This book provides the information you need

to learn what skill areas the tests measure, what general skills your child is being taught in a particular grade, how to prepare your child to take the tests, and what to do with the results. In the appendices you will find information to help you decipher test interpretations; a listing of which states currently require what tests; and additional resources to help you help your child to do better in school and to prepare for the tests.

## A Word about Coaching

This guide is *not* about coaching your child. When we use the term *coaching* in referring to standardized testing, we mean trying to give someone an unfair advantage, either by revealing beforehand what exact items will be on the test or by teaching "tricks" that will supposedly allow a student to take advantage of some detail in how the tests are constructed.

Some people try to coach students in shrewd test-taking strategies that take advantage of how the tests are supposedly constructed rather than strengthening the students' skills in the areas tested. Over the years, for example, many rumors have been floated about "secret formulas" that test companies use.

This type of coaching emphasizes ways to help students obtain scores they didn't earn—to get something for nothing. Stories have appeared in the press about teachers who have coached their students on specific questions, parents who have tried to obtain advance copies of tests, and students who have written down test questions after taking standardized tests and sold them to others. Because of the importance of test security, test companies and states aggressively prosecute those who attempt to violate test security—and they should do so.

## How to Raise Test Scores

Factors that are unrelated to how strong students are but that might artificially lower test scores include anything that prevents students from making scores that accurately describe their actual abilities. Some of those factors are:

- giving the tests in uncomfortably cold or hot rooms;

- allowing outside noises to interfere with test taking; and

- reproducing test booklets in such small print or with such faint ink that students can't read the questions.

Such problems require administrative attention from both the test publishers, who must make sure that they obtain their norms for the tests under the same conditions students face when they take the tests; and school administrators, who must ensure that conditions under which their students take the tests are as close as possible to those specified by the test publishers.

Individual students also face problems that can artificially lower their test scores, and parents can do something about many of these problems. Stomach aches, headaches, sleep deprivation, colds and flu, and emotional upsets due to a recent tragedy are problems that might call for the student to take the tests during make-up sessions. Some students have physical conditions such as muscle-control problems, palsies, or difficulty paying attention that require work over many months or even years before students can obtain accurate test scores on standardized tests. And, of course, some students just don't take the testing seriously or may even intentionally perform poorly. Parents can help their children overcome many of these obstacles to obtaining accurate scores.

Finally, with this book parents are able to help their children raise their scores by:

- increasing their familiarity (and their comfort level) with the types of questions on standardized tests;

- drills and practice exercises to increase their skill in handling the kinds of questions they will meet; and

- providing lots of fun ways for parents to help their children work on the skill areas that will be tested.

## Test Questions

The favorite type of question for standardized tests is the multiple-choice question. For example:

1. The first President of the United States was:

   A  Abraham Lincoln

   B  Martin Luther King, Jr.

   C  George Washington

   D  Thomas Jefferson

The main advantage of multiple-choice questions is that it is easy to score them quickly and accurately. They lend themselves to optical scanning test forms, on which students fill in bubbles or squares and the forms are scored by machine. Increasingly, companies are moving from paper-based testing to computer-based testing, using multiple-choice questions.

The main disadvantage of multiple-choice questions is that they restrict test items to those that can be put in that form. Many educators and civil rights advocates have noted that the multiple-choice format only reveals a superficial understanding of the subject. It's not possible with multiple-choice questions to test a student's ability to construct a detailed, logical argument on some issue or to explain a detailed process. Although some of the major tests are beginning to incorporate more subjectively scored items, such as short answer or essay questions, the vast majority of test items continue to be in multiple-choice format.

In the past, some people believed there were special formulas or tricks to help test-takers determine which multiple-choice answer was the correct one. There may have been some truth to *some* claims for past tests. Computer analyses of some past tests revealed certain biases in how tests were constructed. For example, the old advice to pick *D* when in doubt appears to have been valid for some past tests. However, test publishers have become so sophisticated in their ability to detect patterns of bias in the formulation of test questions and answers that they now guard against it aggressively.

In Chapter 1, we provide information about general test-taking considerations, with advice on how parents can help students overcome testing obstacles. The rest of the book provides information to help parents help their children strengthen skills in the tested areas.

Joseph Harris, Ph.D.

# Test-Taking Basics

**W**elcome to fifth grade! Depending on the structure of your school district, your child may be in the last or next-to-last year of elementary school. As some of the oldest students in the elementary grades, fifth graders are often given extra responsibilities as hall monitors, media center aides, or officers in the Student Council. They also have more opportunities to spend time with friends and away from parents, such as on overnight field trips, traveling with a sports team, or on a class weekend away to build team skills. Your fifth grader is slowly beginning to emerge from a family-centered life to take up a place in a larger social environment.

Many fifth graders take standardized achievement tests like those discussed in the introduction to assess how the district stacks up in comparison to other schools. It's also becoming increasingly likely that your child may take a high-stakes test to determine whether he or she is ready to move on to middle school. Whatever the situation in your school district, your child is becoming more independent and meeting more challenges in life.

## The Fifth Grader's Development

Your fifth grader is rapidly developing the ability to think abstractly as well as on a concrete level. What exactly does that mean? Let's take an easy example. If you ask a kindergartner how a pencil and a crayon are alike, he'll probably tell you that they aren't alike—they're different! If he is even willing to entertain such a silly question from a grown-up, he might concede that both are yellow. A second grader is quickly able to see that there are similarities between the pencil and the crayon, but the similarities are concrete qualities the child can see: They are both held in the hand, both make marks or writing, and both are shaped the same. Your fifth grader will be able to group the crayon and the pencil into an abstract category: writing utensils. He'll be able to tell you the similarities and then easily shift to identifying the essential differences.

In school, your fifth grader will be able to answer "compare and contrast" questions. For example, he can compare and contrast types of precipitation. He can tell you that all types of precipitation are water, but then quickly shift to give the differences between rain, snow, hail, and fog. This mental flexibility and the ability to consider abstract qualities are the basis for the kind of thinking that will be needed in high school and college. Compared to his preschool siblings, your fifth grader is on a different plane when it comes to thinking skills.

Rapidly developing language is a hallmark of this age. Fifth graders are capable of learning many vocabulary words and expanding on what they already know. The shift to abstract thinking makes it possible for them to understand words like *development* or *proficiency*. You can't draw pictures of these words, but children can use words they already know to become familiar with newer, more abstract words. Children of this age are often delighted with the study of words and relish learning new and important-sounding words.

Fifth graders are also capable of understanding exceptions to rules, because of their increased mental flexibility. When young children are developing language, they apply rules rigidly. When little children learn the rule that we add "s" to make plurals in English, they follow the rule universally, making *womans, mouses,* and *childs.* Older children calmly accept the idea of irregular plurals. They understand the need for evaluating information in math problems and using only the relevant facts, rather than adding all the numbers in the problem. When they read stories about Dr. Martin Luther King or Samuel Adams, they can now understand that people should not obey unjust laws or accept unjust taxes just to follow the rules.

Perhaps the greatest development in children at this age is their expanding social environment. The peer group is becoming increasingly important to your child, and he will seek more opportunities to interact with his friends outside the family. In school, he will relish working on projects in groups. He also wants to be seen as competent by his peers, both at home and in school. If your child is having difficulty in school, his sense of competence is at risk. It doesn't matter how many compliments you give your children; a child knows whether he's doing well in school or not.

If you want to build your child's positive view of himself, try helping him to master the skills needed in school by being involved in his school activities. Your child's self-esteem will grow when he is doing well in school and making friends.

## Test-Taking Skills Your Child Needs

A child can't do well on a test if he doesn't know the basics that will be included in the exam. You'll need to build your child's skills in the areas of vocabulary, reading comprehension, language mechanics and expression, spelling, math concepts, application, and computation if

he is to do well on standardized tests. Specific recommendations for skill-building are given in the chapters that follow.

However, a child can have satisfactory knowledge skills and still perform poorly on tests because he lacks test-taking skills. The test-taking skills your child will need are: following directions, managing time limits, managing answer sheets, answering essay questions, and managing anxiety.

### Following Directions

The ability to follow instructions is critical in doing well on any standardized test. Stress the importance of reading all the directions before beginning the test. You can reinforce this skill when your child is doing homework by insisting that your child read the directions aloud before beginning an assignment. If your child doesn't understand the questions, he should be assertive and ask for more explanation.

On some tests, teachers are allowed to repeat directions or even paraphrase to be sure the student understands the questions. Tell your child that the only foolish question is the question that isn't asked! You might remind the child, for example, that some very similar-looking questions ask for synonyms and other questions ask for antonyms. The good test-taker reminds himself of the task while he is working, to avoid making careless mistakes.

### Managing Time Limits

Time management can be tough for fifth graders. Children aren't always aware of the passage of time, and they often do a poor job of estimating how long it will take to complete a task. When they take a test, they may misjudge the amount of time they can spend on questions and end up not even trying many items. Usually, any question left blank will be counted as a wrong answer. Here are some smart testing tips that may help your child:

1.  Listen carefully as the teacher gives directions to determine how much time is allot-

ted for the section. Be sure you know when time will be called.

2. At the beginning of each test section, quickly scan the section to get an idea of how many items there are.

3. Go through the section quickly, answering the questions that you are positive you know. Test questions aren't always arranged in order of difficulty, so don't panic if you find some tough items early in the section.

4. Now work your way through the section a second time. If you find a question that seems difficult, don't get stuck. Put a light checkmark in the margin and simply skip the item.

5. If you have time left after the second round, return to the checked items. If you can eliminate any of the choices, do so. Then make a guess from the remaining answers.

## Managing Answer Sheets

Most standardized tests for fifth graders require students to enter their answers on bubble sheets after reading questions from the test booklet. Sometimes children mistakenly skip a line and end up with incorrectly aligned answers, all of which will be marked wrong. *Tell your child to develop the habit of checking the question number and the answer number at the bottom of each column before beginning the next column of work.* This will help your child discover a skipped line when there is still time to correct the answers.

## Answering Essay Questions

Most standardized tests are largely objective, asking your child to choose the right answer from four options. However, some districts include brief essay questions requiring short answers of several sentences, or even a paragraph or two, to evaluate whether children are developing good writing skills.

In the answers to essay questions, the student is expected to include a topic sentence, a few supporting points, and a conclusion. The best technique is for the child to write a short outline before beginning his composition. Taking a few minutes to jot down a few words is an excellent investment of time to ensure a well-organized essay answer.

Let's imagine that your child is to write a paragraph on the importance of the expeditions of Lewis and Clark. He could begin by jotting down at least three ideas that he considered important about the explorers and their journeys:

- They collected samples of animal and plant life.

- They made a map.

- They met many tribes.

Then the child can write his topic sentence, which is usually the first sentence: "The expedition of Lewis and Clark was important because they discovered new information about the Northwest Territory bought by President Jefferson." Next, he can write sentences using the ideas he listed to describe the new information. He might end the paragraph by giving his own opinion of the expedition. By using this simple outline, the young writer will impress the reader with his organizational skills.

## Managing Anxiety

Let's face it: Most people experience a mild amount of anxiety before any important measure of performance, whether it's a professional play-off game or a standardized test in the fifth grade. In fact, a little anxiety is good for us. It helps us concentrate our energies on the task and do our best. Anxiety is one way that we arouse our energies to surmount an obstacle.

Think back to your own school days. If you had a final exam in two days, your anxiety grew until you just had to sit down and study to make yourself feel more prepared for the test. If friends wanted you to go out for a pizza, you probably had an uncomfortable feeling in your stomach and decided to skip the outing. That exam was too close and you still had a lot of material to review.

Don't become too concerned if your child feels some anxiety about a standardized test he's going to take in fifth grade. If his performance on the test has some important consequence for the child—like repeating the grade or attending summer school—you should wonder about a child who seems not the slightest bit concerned. A child who is unconcerned about a high-stakes test might not understand what is at stake.

On the other hand, some students become so anxious about test performance that they are immobilized and can't demonstrate the skills they have mastered on the test. By fifth grade, you should have noticed whether your child is overly test-anxious. Now is an excellent time to work on the problem, so that your child becomes a good test-taker long before the important tests of high school and college. If you are not sure whether your child's anxiety level is helpful or harmful, look for these signs:

- Your child talks about the test long before it occurs and mentions it frequently.
- Your child reports having difficulty sleeping at night.
- Your child reports "blanking out" on a test when you were reasonably sure that he knew the material.

If you believe your child is unduly test-anxious, there are several techniques you can teach your child to help him cope with his anxiety.

## You're Not Alone

First, tell your child some stories about familiar adults who may have had the same feelings. Children usually love to hear about the school days of their parents, aunts and uncles, or grandparents. Did any relatives or friends have a similar problem that they overcame? Just learning that he isn't the first person in the world to feel anxious about test-taking can help the child put away his fears.

## Visualize Success

Second, help the child learn to play the "inner game" of test-taking. Many Olympic and professional athletes learn to harness their brain power to enhance performance. For example, athletes are taught to visualize themselves executing a play perfectly. Psychologists believe this helps the person execute the activity automatically, without anxiety, in the real-life situation. Your child can learn to use this technique in the classroom. Here's how it works:

- About a week before the test, have your child lie comfortably in bed with his eyes closed.
- Tell him to visualize himself in the classroom, waiting for the teacher to pass out the test booklets. Ask him to try to make this inner picture as vivid as possible, including details of the room and the faces of his classmates.
- Ask him to imagine himself as a confident student who is eager to get the test booklet and show just how well he can do on the test.
- Ask him to look at himself carefully reading the directions and confidently looking for the easy items first.
- Ask him to see himself returning to the harder questions and carefully making his choices with the attitude that he is doing his best.
- If he has trouble seeing himself as a confident person, have him breathe in and out slowly several times until he feels relaxed. If your child is really anxious, have him tense all his muscles and then slowly release them, feeling the relaxation of letting all that tension go.

When your child is relaxed and can imagine himself taking a test confidently, have him form an "anchor"—a reminder to be relaxed. One simple anchor is to press together his thumb and pointer finger. If he becomes anxious during the test, he can form his anchor to remind himself to relax and practice his good test-taking habits.

### Keep Calm

Naturally, you'll want to mark the testing days on your calendar. Try to have a calm week during this time. Don't schedule a trip to the mall to buy jeans the night before the test. Don't have your child's friends over after school, and don't have company from out of town. The night before the test, have dinner, follow your usual family routines, read, and get to bed on time.

The morning of the test, make a special effort to have a pleasant start to the day and be sure your child eats a good breakfast. Even if you have given in to sugared cereals and Pop Tarts in the past, on this morning give your child a breakfast with some protein to provide some sustained energy for that day. Children might love to have a protein-rich fruit shake as something a little special for the big day.

If you make these preparations, your child will unconsciously realize that you value his good performance in school; because you love him, you're willing to provide something special on a stressful day.

### Laugh!

Never overlook the power of humor as an anxiety-buster. It's hard to be nervous when you're laughing. When your child worries about passing the test, counter with humor: "All right, I know this test is a big deal and you're worried about it. But what's the worst that can happen? Is the principal going to pull out your toenails with a pair of pliers? Will you be sent to live in Zanzibar with only peanut butter and grass to eat? Will we have to sell our house and move to the South Pole?"

Finally, check your own perspective. Some parents become so enmeshed in their child's life that they see every test as a reflection of *them,* not their child. Did your son misalign his answer sheet and end up with a long list of incorrect answers, placing him in the first percentile? It's not the end of the world. This is just one measure in a long series of tests that will be used to assess your child's performance.

## How You Can Help Your Child

This book provides specific strategies to help your child become a better test-taker. It also includes tips and ideas for helping your child to develop skills in the areas where you may have identified a weakness. Each chapter discusses a main skill area tested on the fifth-grade levels of the major achievement tests. Testing-type exercises are given throughout the chapter so you and your child can see what to expect. You can also give your child some practice test sessions, if you like.

Some words of advice to parents are in order before we get into the specific skill areas. In most families, one or two parents work outside the home. Many moms and dads race home from a full day at work to begin their "real" job: nurturing their children. But most parents are already tired as they cook supper, wash another load of clothes, and run out to the store to buy yet another sheet of poster board for the social studies project due next week (or more likely, tomorrow!).

By fifth grade, children often have schedules of their own. They may play on a sports team, attend religious classes, or take viola lessons. If there are one or more siblings, the time requirements increase exponentially. When in the world can a parent teach test-taking techniques or tutor a child who is weak in reading comprehension?

Being a realistic working mother and long-time observer of children in schools, I know that parents never have enough time, for themselves or for their children. Many parents hope their children will do their homework in the afternoons. They may sign the homework folder, but often don't look at what the child did or didn't do. By the time their children are in fifth grade, many parents ask if they can't begin to back off a little from close supervision of homework.

I've often heard teachers of fifth graders advise parents to do just that. "Allow your child to experience the natural consequences of not doing homework," they say. "After all, a ten-year-old should certainly be responsible for his own homework. If he doesn't learn to work independently now, what will he do in middle school or high school?"

The words *back off* don't come easily to my lips as a parent. I have seen many parents back off from involvement in their children's school-work, with disastrous results. While the child is supposedly experiencing the natural consequences of a bad grade, the child is also failing to practice skills and falling farther behind in the expected curriculum. I have also noticed that teachers are expected to cram more and more into the curriculum covered in each grade. AIDS education, bully-proofing the classroom, and expanded science and social studies have been added to the upper elementary grade curricula—but nothing has been taken out. As a result, teachers depend more and more on parents to assist with the practice work: learning the times tables, practicing legible cursive handwriting, or learning the vocabulary and spelling words for the week.

Most parents remember doing these activities in school when they were in fifth grade, but there is precious little time left to practice in today's busy school days. Teachers are trying to cover a wide curriculum. Like it or not, you need to be an active partner in your child's education.

Education is not something the teacher gives your child. You are your child's first and most important teacher. If you commit to a reasonable program of study with your child, you will teach him a lot more than the answer to a long-division problem. You will teach a love of learning, the importance of a work ethic, and the need to strive to attain your goals. Even more, you'll learn a lot! You'll learn how your child's mind works, what he enjoys, and what is pure heartache for him. You'll watch him react as you open another wonderful book. You'll learn about his day, about his teacher, and about his friends.

Save the backing off for high school. Savor every day of your child's fifth-grade year. Senior proms will be here before you know it.

Since parents and children have limited amounts of time available for learning after school, and homework takes up a certain amount of that time, when can you fit in the suggested activities in this book?

You're in control three times of the day when your child is at this age: at the supper table, driving in the car, and the last 30 minutes before bedtime. If you commit to spending these times with your child every school day, you can probably work in all the activities in this book. It's very important for children to have a stable daily routine so they feel secure and can learn to plan and manage time. By utilizing these three segments of the day, you can provide anchors in your child's day.

You probably already have a morning routine, especially if you work outside the home. Mornings should be devoted to having breakfast and getting ready for school with a minimum amount of chaos. Clothes, bookbags, and lunches should be ready the night before so that homework, field trip permissions, and projects aren't forgotten. Morning is not the time to work with your child on academic skills.

After school, you may expect your child to get his homework done without your supervision and before taking part in extracurricular activities. Then if you drive him to soccer practice or a scout meeting, you can use this time to play some of the math and word games you'll find in the coming chapters.

Suppertime is the most important time of the day for interaction with your school-aged child. Many busy parents don't have family suppers anymore. Families eat out, or eat in shifts, or just grab something to eat one at a time. This is a terrible mistake. A few years ago, a research study investigated National Merit Scholars to find out what accounted for their sterling performance on standardized tests. Surprisingly, the only thing all these students had in common was that they reported having more family meals than the others!

If you aren't eating together as a family, strongly consider making a commitment to do so at least four times a week. If your child's extracurricular activities or your work schedule doesn't allow the family to eat together, think about what you can change to make family meals a reality in your family. If you don't want to cook, buy take-out food; but do assemble the family for dinner. If one parent can't make it, the other parent can carry the load, or possibly the parents can share the commitment if both work.

Once you carve out this family time, make the most of it. Use the time to teach good manners and discuss interesting news. Let each family member tell about her day. Try some of the vocabulary activities suggested later in this book. Talk to your children and listen to them. Doing this is an investment in their futures and an anchor for the present. It teaches them that family is a priority in your life and should be a priority in theirs.

After supper, look at your children's homework if it was done before you arrived home. Be sure it's done properly. Look for areas where your child might be struggling. If math computation is consistently a problem, turn to Chapter 8 and try some of the suggestions found there. If your child is irresponsible about doing home-work, have him begin to do homework at the kitchen table while you are doing dishes, making lunches, paying bills, or reading the paper. Turn off the television and create a quiet, studious atmosphere in the house. Don't allow telephone conversations while homework is being done. As the children complete their homework, allow them to leave the room to take their showers and get ready for the next day. Then they can enjoy themselves. This will serve as an incentive to get homework done.

The last anchor of the day should be the final 30 minutes before bedtime, when you read aloud to your children. This should be a relaxing, enjoyable, and warm family time. Many researchers have found that children who are read to become good readers and have large vocabularies. A quiet reading time also acts as an excellent transition from the evening, to help the child get settled and ready to sleep. You'll find more information about selecting books and how to read aloud to your child in Chapter 2. The most important thing is for you to commit to this activity, night after night, during your child's elementary and middle school years.

Now that you know how to set up your day to maximize your child's chances for academic success, let's move ahead to the tests and what your child will be expected to know. Activities will be recommended that will fit into your anchor times of commuting time, suppertime, and bedtime.

# CHAPTER 2

# Vocabulary

One of the greatest gifts you can give to your children is to help them build vocabulary. Not only will it help on standardized tests taken in fifth grade, but it will help them on all the important tests to be faced in the future: high school entrance exams, high school exit exams, and college entrance tests.

Having an extensive vocabulary makes reading more pleasurable, helps your child express herself better, and gives us all an appreciation of the richness of our language. A person with a broad vocabulary writes better cover letters for business purposes, sounds better at important social occasions, and even writes a better love letter to a future spouse! To help your child prepare for tests and perform better overall in school, begin by enriching her vocabulary knowledge.

## What You and Your Child Can Do

There are a hundred ways every day that you can boost your child's vocabulary, if only you're aware of them. Here are a few ideas:

### Talk

The first important tip in developing vocabulary is to spend time talking with your child. Try to use precise language to express yourself to your children, and avoid vague words like *stuff* or *things*.

"Caitlin, please bring the silverware to set the table" is much more precise than "Bring that stuff over to the table."

### Teachable Moments

As you talk, be alert for that little puzzled look in your child's eyes when you use an unfamiliar word. Either explain what you've said, or ask if your child knows the word in question. "Jane, could you hand me the cutlery? You know, that means *knives*."

When you are driving and listening to the radio, be alert for unfamiliar words in commercials or songs. Ask your child to guess what the word means, provide a definition if necessary, and then use the word in another sentence so the child can pick up the flavor of how we use the word in our language.

YOU: Did you hear the weather reporter say that it's going to be a *dreary* day? What do you think that means, *a dreary day*?

CHILD: I dunno. Maybe *dreary* like *cleary*?

YOU: No, a dreary day is a gloomy day, maybe gloomy because the sun doesn't come out and it's cloudy and cold. We might also say that a story is dreary if it is sad and depressing, but we'd probably never say that a car is dreary, even if it is old and dilapidated.

CHILD: What does *dilapidated* mean?

As you can see, this conversation could go on and on!

### Daily Reading

Another great source of vocabulary words for your child is her daily reading, whether it's books for schoolwork or for pleasure. Many parents read daily to preschoolers, but that daily interaction begins to peter out as the child learns to read for herself.

This is a great loss for the child—and for you, too! When you stop reading to your child, you lose the chance to learn about your child's interests and schoolwork. Your child misses out on your example as a reader and loses hundreds of chances to learn new words easily and in context.

I recommend reading to your child at bedtime for at least 20 minutes, four nights a week. Read with your child as far into middle school as possible, or even into high school, if you come upon a book that you know your teenager would enjoy. This should be a warm and relaxing part of your day. If you're tired after working hard, let your child read some pages to you. If your child is tired, you do all the reading that evening. Always pause when you come to a word you think your child might not know. Offer quick definitions so that you don't spoil the pleasure of the story.

**Look It Up!** Many parents are concerned that they may not know the meanings of words when they read higher-level books to their fifth graders. There's no need for embarrassment: You can be a good role model by admitting that you don't know the word and have to look it up in the dictionary yourself. You've just shown your child that you are a lifelong learner too.

**Find Good Books.** Parents can play an invaluable role in encouraging vocabulary building and reading skills in their children by finding great books for their children to read. Remember that you are your child's first teacher, and you probably know your child better than any other adult on earth. You know what interests her, what captivates her, and what bores her. Pay attention to what books she likes and try to find other books by the same author or books on similar themes. Find out which books are popular in the world of children's literature, and sample some of these.

Your local librarian can recommend popular selections, or you can check out Web sites that review children's books (see Appendix A).

If a book bores you or your child, stop reading and return it to the library! Ideally, the books you select should be so wonderful that both you and your child would be disappointed if you had to skip your reading time one rare evening. If you choose books that are stimulating, humorous, or suspenseful, you'll see both reading skill and vocabulary increase at a very quick pace.

### Word Challenge

Besides reading frequently with and to your child, there is another great technique to build a good vocabulary rapidly: Ask your child to tell you one new word each day, and have her use the word correctly in a sentence. This can be done at the supper table before everyone gets up to clear the table. You'll be amazed at the progress your child will make in a few weeks.

## What Tests May Ask

No matter which standardized test your child will take this year, chances are she'll be asked about:

- Basic vocabulary
- Synonyms
- Antonyms
- Words with more than one meaning
- Words in context
- Word study

Read on to find more information about each of these topics, what your child will be expected to know, and how you can help.

### Basic Vocabulary

Standardized tests will assess your child's basic word knowledge. The questions are usually multiple-choice types that ask the child to choose the answer most like the definition of an indicated word. The items test a wide range of words, from familiar words to challenging ones.

## What Your Fifth Grader Should Be Learning

Fifth graders should be able to decode or sound out most words on the tests. Basic vocabulary items usually present the target word embedded in a phrase, so the student can also glean some clue as to the meaning of the word from the context of the phrase.

## What You Can Do

If you follow the tips discussed earlier in this chapter, your child's basic vocabulary should increase from family conversations, family reading time, and new words discussed at the dinner table.

Many researchers agree that the most effective path to building vocabulary is reading. Read, read, read—with your child and to your child. Also, be sure your child is independently reading books at her own reading level.

If you're concerned that your child is reading books that may be too hard for her, ask the child's teacher for a general estimate of the child's independent reading level. The independent level is the level at which a child can read without help and still understand at least 85 percent of the material. A child's instructional level is the level at which the child is taught in the classroom. At the instructional level, the child needs some adult help to sound out some words and also to understand the material.

The teacher can determine a child's independent reading level by having the child read a passage and answer questions about what she's read. Many schools use computer programs that can assess the independent reading level in the same way.

When you know your child's independent reading level, ask the children's specialist at your local public library to help you locate appropriate books.

## Practice Skills: Basic Vocabulary

**Directions:** Read each item. Choose the answer that means the same or about the same as the underlined word.

1 a catastrophic storm
- Ⓐ beneficial
- Ⓑ disastrous
- Ⓒ severe
- Ⓓ mild

2 a decent man
- Ⓐ horrible
- Ⓑ crafty
- Ⓒ well-dressed
- Ⓓ respectable

3 a cozy cottage
- Ⓐ snug
- Ⓑ chilly
- Ⓒ pretty
- Ⓓ hot

4 pursue your dreams
- Ⓐ sleep through
- Ⓑ forget
- Ⓒ follow
- Ⓓ remember

5 a deserted habitation
- Ⓐ form of clothing
- Ⓑ a place where people used to work
- Ⓒ an abode
- Ⓓ a shack

(See page 101 for answer key.)

### Synonyms and Antonyms

The tests your child will take usually include a section on synonyms (words that have the same meanings) and antonyms (words with opposite meanings). Again, these questions will be presented in a multiple-choice format.

## What Your Fifth Grader Should Be Learning

The middle childhood years are when a child develops depth in her language. She now knows more than one way to say that a scene is pretty (synonyms) and she has the intellectual resources to figure out the opposite of a given word (antonyms).

## What You Can Do

Children like to learn unusual words that sound important, but your child might find the terms *synonym* and *antonym* confusing. If the child confuses the terms, she'll do badly on this section of the standardized test. Remind your child that *synonym* and *same* both start with the letter *s. Anti* means *against*; antonyms are two words whose meanings "go against" each other.

When you're teaching definitions at the supper table, in the car, or during family reading time, you usually give the child simpler or more familiar synonyms. A good teacher always uses a bridge from what the child knows to help her leap to what is unknown.

To teach antonyms, play the game "Opposites" when you are driving or waiting in line with your children. The first player says a word; the player who can give an opposite word or antonym first gets one point and the chance to call out the next word.

## Practice Skills: Synonyms

**Directions:** Read each item. Choose the word that means the same or about the same as the underlined word.

6  comrade
- Ⓐ  enemy
- Ⓑ  stranger
- Ⓒ  acquaintance
- Ⓓ  friend

7  fidget
- Ⓐ  move around nervously
- Ⓑ  a gadget
- Ⓒ  to lie
- Ⓓ  a sweet candy

8  distinguish
- Ⓐ  to put out a fire
- Ⓑ  to disgrace
- Ⓒ  to recognize the differences
- Ⓓ  to wash

9  passive
- Ⓐ  active
- Ⓑ  lacking energy
- Ⓒ  smiling
- Ⓓ  unhappy

10  interval
- Ⓐ  in front
- Ⓑ  a valley
- Ⓒ  a time between two events
- Ⓓ  inside the body

(See page 101 for answer key.)

## Practice Skills: Antonyms

**Directions:** Read each item. Choose the answer that means the opposite of the underlined word.

11  saccharine
- Ⓐ  very sweet
- Ⓑ  loud
- Ⓒ  frightening
- Ⓓ  sour

12  notorious
- Ⓐ  acclaimed
- Ⓑ  sinister
- Ⓒ  evil
- Ⓓ  helpful

**13** gloomy

    Ⓐ  depressing

    Ⓑ  cheerful

    Ⓒ  unhappy

    Ⓓ  sticky

**14** flourish

    Ⓐ  flower

    Ⓑ  submerge

    Ⓒ  decline

    Ⓓ  polish

**15** accelerate

    Ⓐ  climb up

    Ⓑ  slow down

    Ⓒ  speed up

    Ⓓ  maintain the same speed

(See page 101 for answer key.)

## Multi-Meaning Words

Standardized tests usually include a section of words with more than one meaning. Using context clues from the rest of the sentence, the child has to choose which meaning of the word is being used in that sentence.

## What Your Fifth Grader Should Be Learning

Your fifth grader should understand that words have multiple meanings. She should be adept at using the context to help her figure out which meaning is being used. She should also have had practice in eliminating some of the choices given and taking an educated guess if she is not completely sure of the right answer.

## What You Can Do

Children in the fifth grade usually love to play games with words. They are fascinated by words that look unusual, sound different, or seem grown-up. You can play a word game using words with multiple meanings.

Have each player list a word with two or more distinct meanings and use the word in two different sentences to show the meanings. Players get one point for coming up with a word with two meanings, and a bonus point for each meaning beyond that. A round of the game might sound like this:

CHILD: My word is *paint*. You could say that you painted the outside of the house, but paint is also a material.

YOU: What's your sentence for the second meaning?

CHILD: The artist made his own paint from berries and oil.

YOU: Good for you! You get one point. My word, *cut*, has three meanings.

CHILD: Three meanings? I can only think of two.

YOU: Well, we could say that I *cut* an orange into four pieces, or you could say that you put a bandaid on your *cut*.

CHILD: That's only two meanings. There aren't any more!

YOU: Well, you might not know this meaning, but a cut can also mean an insult. Here's my sentence: The boy made an unkind *cut* about the bully's size. So I've earned one point for my first two meanings and a bonus point for the third meaning!

Your child may say that it's not fair to compete against someone with a larger vocabulary, but children of this age are very competitive. You'll be surprised at how quickly your child will scout out other words to stump you.

## Practice Skills: Multi-Meaning Words

**Directions:** Read each item. Choose the sentence (A or B) in which the underlined word has the same meaning as the underlined word in the sample sentence:

**16** The great <u>pitcher</u> was chosen for the All-Star team.

   Ⓐ  The <u>pitcher</u> was filled with lemonade.

   Ⓑ  The <u>pitcher</u> had great control of the baseball.

**17** I keep my homework in a <u>file.</u>

   Ⓐ  The secretary put the papers in a <u>file.</u>

   Ⓑ  The manicurist used a <u>file</u> to smooth my nails.

**18** The teacher's <u>pen</u> ran out of ink.

   Ⓐ  I like to write with a <u>pen.</u>
   Ⓑ  The sheep are standing in the <u>pen.</u>

**19** I have a red <u>comb</u> for my hair.

   Ⓐ  The bees store honey in a <u>comb.</u>

   Ⓑ  Her <u>comb</u> and brush were on the dresser.

(See page 101 for answer key.)

## Words in Context

Many tests require children to find words in context. In this type of task, the child is given a sentence with a missing word, followed by four choices. The student must choose the word that best completes the sentence.

## What Your Fifth Grader Should Be Learning

If your child has a broad vocabulary and is surrounded by adults who talk to her, she'll usually have no difficulty finding the appropriate choice. By this age, children should be used to making educated guesses on tests, trying out answers to see which one sounds right, and using the context to decide which words make sense.

## What You Can Do

You can help your child sharpen this skill during your evening reading sessions. Before you turn each page, have your child guess what the first word on the next page will be. You'll be amazed at how adept a child can be at predicting the words of a familiar author.

When you're reading aloud, you can simply pause and have your child predict the next word to be read. In the practice exercise, you may notice that your child has difficulty juggling so many choices. Teach your child to skim or read the entire passage quickly to get some general idea of the paragraph. Then take the sentences in order and try out the most reasonable choices. Lightly pencil in the first choices. If the paragraph begins to sound like nonsense, return to an earlier choice and try another option. *The key to being successful on this type of task is to stay flexible in your thinking.*

## Practice Skills: Words in Context

**Directions:** Read the paragraph. Below the paragraph are seven groups of numbered word choices. Choose the correct word that fits into the numbered blanks.

How much do you know about the common cold? It is an 20._____ characterized by a stuffy nose, sneezing, cough, and sore throat. The 21._____ cold is usually spread by 22._____ contact with a sick person. However, you can pick up the viruses by touching hard surfaces like doorknobs or telephones that are infected by the virus.

There are ways you can 23._____ getting a cold. You can practice good eating 24._____, exercise 25._____, and wash your hands 26._____ during cold season.

**20**  Ⓐ  illness
     Ⓑ  habit
     Ⓒ  character
     Ⓓ  condition

21  Ⓐ terrible
    Ⓑ common
    Ⓒ mild
    Ⓓ severe

22  Ⓐ touching
    Ⓑ average
    Ⓒ direct
    Ⓓ little

23  Ⓐ improve
    Ⓑ help
    Ⓒ increase
    Ⓓ avoid

24  Ⓐ foods
    Ⓑ weekly
    Ⓒ help
    Ⓓ habits

25  Ⓐ regularly
    Ⓑ occasionally
    Ⓒ sometimes
    Ⓓ anytime

26  Ⓐ rarely
    Ⓑ frequently
    Ⓒ never
    Ⓓ sometimes

(See page 101 for answer key.)

## Word Study

Some standardized tests include words that require students to understand that words in our language come from many other languages. In addition, the students should know that certain parts of words can give us a clue as to the meaning of the words.

# What Your Fifth Grader Should Be Learning

Your child should have had plenty of practice at looking up words in a dictionary and should have noticed that the origins of many words are given in the entries. She should also be able to identify common prefixes, suffixes, and roots in English words.

# What You Can Do

If your child seems unfamiliar with root words, prefixes, suffixes, or the origins of words, don't be too concerned. This may not be part of the curriculum in your school and it isn't a major part of any standardized test.

**Get a Good Dictionary.** Learning about words will be a tremendous help on tests your child will take in the future, and it's also a fun, interesting way to expand her vocabulary. If you don't have a good dictionary, buy one. Your child will need a good dictionary for high school and college assignments, even if she does all her spell-checking on a word processing program.

## Prefixes and Suffixes

As you are going over vocabulary words at the table after meals or when your child comes upon an unfamiliar word, be aware of any prefixes or suffixes that can help your child figure out the meanings by herself. Here's an example:

CHILD: Mom, I don't know this word—*fictitious*.

YOU: But you know another word that's very close. What's another word that begins with f-i-c-t?

CHILD: Do you mean the word *fiction*?

YOU: Yes. And what does *fiction* mean?

CHILD: A book that isn't true.

YOU: And *fictitious* means anything that isn't true or real. When you see the *ous* at the end of a word, that should tell you that the word is an adjective, like *gorgeous* or *monstrous*. So if I told you that a criminal gave his boss a fictitious address, what would that mean?

CHILD: Oh, I get it. He gave the man a fake address.

## Practice Skills: Word Study

**Directions:** Choose the answer that best defines the underlined part of each word.

**27** <u>anti</u>freeze

  Ⓐ  in favor of
  Ⓑ  between
  Ⓒ  without
  Ⓓ  against

**28** <u>re</u>write

  Ⓐ  take away
  Ⓑ  in favor of
  Ⓒ  opposite
  Ⓓ  do over

**29** Which of these words probably come from the Latin word <u>manus</u>, meaning "hand?"

  Ⓐ  mean
  Ⓑ  manner
  Ⓒ  manual
  Ⓓ  mansion

(See page 101 for answer key.)

# CHAPTER 3

# Reading Comprehension

Reading comprehension tests a child's general ability to understand what a piece of writing is all about, what the author was trying to say, and what the tone of the piece is.

## Goals for Fifth Graders

In fifth grade, your child should be reading a variety of literary forms: poems, nonfiction, essays, myths, plays, autobiographies, and newspaper articles. He should not only be able to read the passages aloud at a steady rate and with good expression, but he should also be able to answer the basic questions about who was in the story, what happened, and when and where the story took place. These are called literal comprehension skills.

However, at this age your child should also be able to branch into critical and inferential reading skills. This means your child should be able to think about what he has read and make some educated guesses about what is implied in the story. Even when the author never directly states an opinion about a certain subject, can your child predict what the author would say about a topic based on what he has already read in a particular passage?

Your child should also be able to distinguish between a fact in the story and the author's opinions. He should be able to make predictions, draw conclusions, and catch inferences; in other words, he has to be able to read between the lines to pick up information about which the author has only hinted.

By this age, your child should be able to name the characters of a story, describe the setting, pick out the main points of the plot, and even describe the genre. Is this a poem? Historical fiction? A biography? A humorous essay? Many parents are surprised that children learn about genre during the elementary grades, but this approach to literature is taught early in many school districts.

## What You and Your Child Can Do

There's no need to feel overwhelmed when it comes to helping your child develop reading comprehension skills. You can work on the most important skills at the same time you do the vocabulary building we discussed in Chapter 2.

When you are reading to your child at night, pause in appropriate places and ask what might happen next to the main character. Besides maintaining the suspense and setting up the next night's installment, asking your child to guess the next scene will help him learn to make predictions. If his answer seems completely off-base to you, ask him to explain his answer. Debate a little, using facts from the story.

Before you begin a new book, read the blurbs from the book jacket to your child. Have him predict what the book will be about. Ask him what kind of a book it is: fiction or nonfiction? biography or autobiography? realistic or fantasy? science fiction or romance? Be sure to choose a variety of books for your nightly reading sessions. A child who has just finished a wonderful book with characters zipping through the universe via time travel will have a clear mental picture of the realistic science fiction genre. The young man who has read a book about one of his favorite sports heroes won't have much difficulty remembering what a biography is.

You can see the importance of nightly family reading. These sessions can teach vocabulary, reading comprehension, and critical thinking skills as you and your child enjoy each other's company and create some wonderful family memories. All working parents are tired at night and are looking for a way to relieve some stress; but don't skip your reading sessions. They are critical for your child's present and future success.

## What Tests May Ask

Standardized tests of reading comprehension will probably test your child on the ability to spot details and pick out information, to trace the main ideas of a story, to draw inferences, and to identify the tone or mood of a story.

### Literal Comprehension

Literal comprehension skills refer to questions that are directly answered in the text. Your child will read passages of varying length and then answer straightforward questions about what he has read.

## What Your Fifth Grader Should Be Learning

Fifth graders should be able to answer questions that ask who is in the story, what happened, when it happened, and what certain words or expressions mean in the story.

In addition, he should be able to identify the basic elements of character, plot, climax, setting, and mood.

## What You Can Do

If your child is having trouble answering literal questions, that's a problem. The most likely cause of failure in this area is that the story is written above your child's independent reading level. In other words, your child is spending so much time trying to sound out the words or figure out what the words mean that he has no mental energy left to think about what the passage means.

Have your child read part of the passage aloud to you. If he's struggling over every fifth word, then the passage is above his reading level. Choose a simpler text and try some literal questions at that level.

Here's another easy test: Read the passage aloud to your child and then ask the questions out loud. If he can answer correctly, that means that his reading is the problem, not his ability to comprehend. If he simply doesn't know what the words mean in the selection, then you have some words to work on at the dinner table.

## What Tests May Ask

In standardized tests of literal comprehension, your child can expect to be presented with a brief passage he must read, and then to answer a series of questions about the passage. The questions are usually straightforward, asking for details about the setting, tone, and chain of events. Often, these tests also ask your child to decide what was *not* included in the sample passage.

## Practice Skills: Literal Comprehension

**Directions:** Read the passage below. Find the best answer to the questions that follow.

Daniel was very excited when the mailman delivered the boxes containing his new computer. First, he carefully unpacked all the components. Next, he read the manual to learn how to assemble the system. Then he moved his table close to a power source and gathered the tools listed in the manual to connect the components. Finally, he began to follow the directions given in the manual.

Soon his bedroom was filled with packing material, parts, tools, and components. It was a mess, but a mess that would be worth all the trouble.

**1** The setting of this story is:
- Ⓐ an office
- Ⓑ a factory
- Ⓒ a bedroom
- Ⓓ a home

**2** What was the first action Daniel took when his computer was delivered?
- Ⓐ He gathered his tools.
- Ⓑ He read the manual.
- Ⓒ He thanked the mailman.
- Ⓓ He unpacked the components.

**3** Which of these is NOT explained in the story?
- Ⓐ How Daniel got ready to assemble his computer
- Ⓑ Who delivered the computer to Daniel
- Ⓒ Who paid for the computer
- Ⓓ Where Daniel set up his computer

(See page 101 for answer key.)

## Critical Reading and Inferential Comprehension

These two comprehension skills refer to thinking about what has been read. These skills include making predictions about what will happen next, separating fact from opinion, drawing inferences, figuring out the meaning of words and phrases used in the passage, and making comparisons.

## What Your Fifth Grader Should Be Learning

A fifth grader should have covered all of the critical reading skills prior to this year. During fifth grade, the student should be improving skills and applying them in more difficult passages. He should read a lot of nonfiction, such as the writing found in science books. This is important because it gets your child ready for history and science textbooks that he'll study in middle school and high school.

## What You Can Do

You can work on critical thinking skills during your nightly reading. Ask questions like:

What do you think will happen next to the main character in the story?

Why do you think the main character decided to take this action rather than doing something else?

If our main character were alive today, how do you think he would feel about the space shuttle missions? How do you know that?

It's also important to reveal your own critical thinking to your child, so he can understand that we read to get the author's opinions, and then either agree or disagree, based on our own experience. Many children never get the chance to hear adults discuss information they read about.

Most of us have limited time to study with our children each day, so make the most of your time at the dinner table. A few times each week, bring to the table a newspaper or magazine article that might interest your child. Most news articles are written at the sixth-grade level, so you might have to define several words or explain some sentences. While you are reading, pause and think aloud about the article. When you are finished, have a family discussion about the content.

Fifth graders are usually idealistic and committed to preserving the environment, so you might select articles about this area. Letters to the editor are another good choice, because they provide a solid source of opinions that may or may not have a relationship to the facts presented.

## What Tests May Ask

Standardized tests of inferential comprehension and critical reading present a sample bit of text followed by a series of questions that require a thoughtful evaluation of the passage. Students may be asked to predict what would happen next, or to manipulate the information to come up with answers to novel questions.

## Practice Skills: Inferential Comprehension and Critical Reading

**Directions:** Read the following paragraph. Then choose the answer you think is correct for each question.

The last dinosaur disappeared from the earth about seventy million years ago, but we know about these fantastic creatures from the fossils they left behind. The word *dinosaur* comes from two Greek words that mean "terrible lizard." We would probably agree that they were terrible lizards if we could travel back in time to see them. The allosaurus was 35 feet long with huge, sharp teeth to attack its prey. The triceratops had three razor-sharp horns on its six-foot-high head to slash its enemies. But as our world changed, the environment became unkind to the dinosaurs. Swamps dried up, trees grew too close together for the huge creatures to move freely, and the food supply began to diminish. One by one, the dinosaurs died off, leaving the world to the mammals, who were much better adapted to live there.

4 Which of the following would be the best title for this story?

- Ⓐ The Dinosaurs
- Ⓑ The Terrible Lizards
- Ⓒ The Disappearance of the Dinosaurs
- Ⓓ The Allosaurus

5 Which of the following is NOT a fact from the story?

- Ⓐ Dinosaurs probably looked terrible.
- Ⓑ Triceratops had three razor-sharp horns.
- Ⓒ Allosaurus was 35 feet long.
- Ⓓ We learn about dinosaurs from fossils.

6 You would probably understand the word *dinosaur* if you could speak

- Ⓐ Spanish
- Ⓑ Greek
- Ⓒ Latin
- Ⓓ Russian

7 Judging by what happened to the dinosaurs, what prediction would you make about life on earth today if we had a sudden, dramatic change in the environment?

- Ⓐ Animal and plant life would go on the same as always.
- Ⓑ Many kinds of animal and plant life would die out.
- Ⓒ The dinosaurs could come back to earth.
- Ⓓ We would find more fossils.

**Directions:** Read the following letter written to a newspaper. Choose the best answer for each of the questions that follow.

To the Editor:

I was furious to read about the wastewater that is being dumped into Lake Lanier. The county officials say that the water has been treated and is safe for the lake, but I just don't believe it. I am a fisherman and I have seen the fish become smaller and less plentiful since the wastewater has been dumped into our lake. Anyone who has a nose can smell the difference in how the lake smells now and how it used to be when I was a boy. I think that some officials are working so closely with some of our businesspeople and developers that they no longer care about what is good for the people of our county. I know where I will be next November fourth—in the voting booth!

**8** The writer of the letter is probably

(A) an environmentalist
(B) a developer
(C) a county official
(D) a hunter

**9** What do you predict that the writer will do in November?

(A) Vote for all the current county officials.

(B) Vote for president.

(C) Vote against all the current county officials.

(D) Stay home.

**10** What is the tone of this letter?

(A) hopeful
(B) angry
(C) reasonable
(D) depressed

**Directions:** Read the following selection and then answer the questions.

My friend Kassie has always been a person of great heart and strength. She is a wonderful nurse in a pediatric ward of a major hospital in our city. One of her patients had an unexpected effect on her life, and also on the lives of Kassie's family and friends. Kassie's patient Jon was a young boy aged 11, who was flown to the United States from Bosnia in an air ambulance. Jon had been walking to visit his grandparents in Bosnia and stepped on an unexploded land mine. He had lost part of his right leg and had suffered many complicated injuries on his other limbs. Because medical care was limited in Bosnia, Jon was flown here for a long series of operations and an even longer period of therapy to see how far he could recover.

When Jon arrived in Kassie's unit, he couldn't speak much English. He was in great physical pain, and was in even more emotional pain from the loss of his leg. Kassie felt great compassion for her young patient, but she knew that Jon would need to work hard if he was going to recover. She decided to combine toughness with a sense of humor to spur Jon on.

The first morning, Jon was lying in bed, staring at the ceiling. His eyes were red and swollen with tears. He looked at Kassie as she came into the room, but showed no interest in her and went back to examining the ceiling. Kassie tried to get his attention, but he didn't respond. She came back into the room with an erasable marker and a whiteboard, and she quickly drew a cartoon horse and a stick figure of a boy.

"Jon, look here!" she said forcefully. No response came.

"Jon, I'm talking to you, and when I talk, people listen!" She put her arms around him and lifted him to a sitting position. "This is you," she said, pointing to the stick figure. She erased the figure and quickly sketched another boy, riding the horse.

"This horse is your body, and you are going to ride that horse. And I am going to be the trainer." She sketched herself with a long rope around the horse. "Understand?"

Jon pushed away the board and angrily turned his head away, but Kassie grabbed his shoulders and pulled him around to face her. She quickly erased the figures and drew the horse with a riding crop on one side, and an apple on the other.

"We can play this any way you like. We can hit the horse with the crop to make him run, or we can promise him a sweet apple to get him to run. But either way, this horse is going to run." With these words, Kassie began to run around the room, pretending to be a horse. She pranced and snorted and whinnied, and soon Jon's mouth was beginning to turn up at the corners. He caught himself and tried to frown, but he was too late. The galloping horse stopped, pawed the floor in front of the bed, and laid its front hoof alongside Jon's leg. The "mare" nuzzled the boy's hand insistently, until the boy gave in and patted Kassie's head. "Aha!" thought Kassie. "I think we may have made the first step."

**11** What is the author's purpose in this passage?

Ⓐ To get money for victims of land mines

Ⓑ To entertain Jon

Ⓒ To describe the nurse's character

Ⓓ To persuade the audience that land mines are evil

**12** What character trait is not true of Kassie from what you have read of her?

Ⓐ generous
Ⓑ funny
Ⓒ compassionate
Ⓓ forceful

**13** What character trait is true of Jon from what you know of him?

Ⓐ athletic
Ⓑ stingy
Ⓒ truthful
Ⓓ angry

**14** What metaphor does Kassie use to communicate with John?

Ⓐ a crop and apple
Ⓑ a horse trainer
Ⓒ a high-spirited mare
Ⓓ all of the above

**15** What do you think will happen next in the story?

Ⓐ Jon will begin his therapy.

Ⓑ Jon will return to Bosnia able to walk with a walker.

Ⓒ Jon will become an American citizen.

Ⓓ Jon will give up on therapy.

(See page 101 for answer key.)

# CHAPTER 4

# Language Mechanics

Language mechanics at the fifth grade level basically refers to punctuation and capitalization. Many parents and students consider language mechanics a boring, painful area of study. But with today's trend toward higher standards and more standardized testing, you can expect that your child will be tested on her knowledge of the mechanics of English.

Most high school teachers expect their students to be proficient in these two areas and deduct credit for mistakes, so advise your fifth grader to learn the mechanics of her own language.

## Education Goals for Fifth Graders

By fifth grade, students are expected to know the uses of the capital letter in all its forms. Punctuation requirements vary from one school district to the next, but a fifth grader should certainly be expert on the use of final punctuation. She should know when to end a sentence with a period, a question mark, or an exclamation mark. Of course, she should know that every sentence has to end with some form of final punctuation.

Fifth graders should also be able to correctly use quotation marks to enclose something that someone said, or to enclose the title of a short work, like a poem or a song. Fifth graders should know how to use commas and periods within quotation marks, and they should be able to use an apostrophe to form a contraction or a possessive. Finally, they should be able to use commas correctly in a series or in an address.

## What You and Your Child Can Do

Language mechanics is becoming an important part of the curriculum in many fifth grade classrooms, now that many schools are experiencing a swing away from a pure "whole language" approach to the language arts. Your child is probably doing punctuation and capitalization on a daily basis in her classroom. Check with your child's teacher to be sure that punctuation and capitalization are being taught. If your district doesn't emphasize this area, you need to act to help your child.

A very popular approach used in many school districts today is called "daily oral language" (DOL). In this approach, the students find two sentences on the board when they enter the room. These sentences contain many errors. The students' task is to rewrite the sentences correctly.

If your district is teaching the mechanics of English, go over your child's homework and classwork that are sent home daily or weekly. Look for errors your child has made and analyze them.

Is your child reliably capitalizing the start of each sentence? The personal pronoun *I*? The names of proper nouns, such as cities, months, and people's names? Titles of individuals as well as titles of books?

If you notice a problem with lack of capitalization that comes up again and again, be sure your child understands how to insert the capitals. Then you can practice "Dinner Table DOL"

GRADE FIVE: GET READY!

each evening before the child leaves the table after supper.

Let's imagine that your child usually forgets to capitalize proper nouns. Give her a sheet of notebook paper on which you have written:

My grandfather came from dayton, ohio.

Have your child correct the errors. When she has gotten a perfect paper on each of four nights, tell her that you are done with Dinner Table DOL until you notice the next error in her classwork.

This lets your child know that you have a healthy interest in her schoolwork, that you value good mechanics, and that she has an incentive for applying the mechanics of English to her daily writing. The goal is for your child to apply capitals and punctuation so automatically that she'll never have to give it a moment's thought in her high school and college writing, thus freeing her energies for creative and organized writing.

If your school district doesn't emphasize capitalization and punctuation in fifth grade, the best advice is to make Dinner Table DOL a nightly part of your life. Your child will be expected to know these skills on standardized tests, and more importantly, in college or on the job. Teach her yourself if this isn't emphasized at her school. Many parents shy away from the idea of teaching grammar at the dinner table, but these are basic concepts: the capital letter, the period, and the comma. No child should be sent into adult life unable to write a correct, coherent sentence.

You can make this activity agreeable for your child. Supply her with colored markers and highlighters to find the errors, and let her earn points for detecting all the errors. Then let her trade in her grammar points to be relieved of a chore or stay up 30 minutes later one school night or earn some other coveted prize.

Another easy strategy is to point out the grammatical errors that are seen on signs everywhere. Children love to feel superior to adults, even if it is knowing that we should write *John's Restaurant* rather than *Johns' Restaurant*!

## Capitalization

Capitalization may seem like a simple concept, but you'd be surprised at the number of times fifth graders slip up on this "simple" grammar point.

## What Your Fifth Grader Should Be Learning

By fifth grade, students are expected to know the uses of the capital letter. This is not complicated: We capitalize the beginning word of a sentence; the personal pronoun *I*; most of the words in titles of books, plays, and movies; and proper nouns, which include names of people, geographical places, days of the week, months, holidays, and religions.

## What You Can Do

Look at your child's writings from school and analyze the errors. If you find that your child is consistently making errors in capitalization, have her correct two sentences daily containing the errors that she commonly makes.

If your child seems to understand capitals, be sure she understands the format of the test items following the section on punctuation. Many children need some practice to get used to the format commonly used on standardized tests.

## Punctuation

No matter how beautifully a piece of writing is composed, if it is littered with punctuation errors, the author ends up looking like a poor writer indeed. Yet many adults make punctuation errors all the time, and are blissfully unaware that their mistakes seriously affect others' opinions of their ability, education, or intelligence.

If an elementary-age child understands and gets used to correctly using punctuation now, it will become automatic in the future. The rules of punctuation are not particularly difficult; with practice, they can become second nature.

## What Your Fifth Grader Should Be Learning

Your fifth grader is expected to know the fine points of punctuation by now, including all the rules for the correct use of a period, comma, question mark, exclamation point, quotation marks, and apostrophe.

## What You Can Do

If you find that you have to do more teaching in this area than you had expected, and you find that you're a little shaky on the basics (many adults are), haunt the used-book stores for old grammar books. They are wonderfully clear. If you can't find anything, buy a college handbook of style at any bookstore (the rules of grammar don't change by grade), or buy an *AP Stylebook* (the punctuation bible for most newspaper and magazine writers).

## Practice Skills: Capitalization and Punctuation

**Directions:** Choose the answer that shows the correct capitalization and punctuation.

1 Our country's birthday is july 4 1776.
   A  July 4, 1776.
   B  July 4 1776.
   C  Correct as is.

2 I was born in morgantown, West virginia.
   A  morgantown, West Virginia.
   B  Morgantown West Virginia
   C  Morgantown, West Virginia.
   D  Correct as is.

3 Martin luther king was a famous civil rights leader.
   A  Martin luther King
   B  Martin Luther King
   C  Correct as is.

4 "I am going to washington for a visit", said Kassie.
   A  "I am going to Washington for a visit". said Kassie.
   B  "I am going to Washington for a visit," said Kassie.
   C  "I am going to Washington for a visit." said Kassie.

5 Louisa may alcott wrote *Little women.*
   A  Louisa May Alcott wrote "Little women."
   B  Louisa May Alcott wrote *Little Women.*
   C  Correct as is.

**Directions:** Choose the letter of the punctuation mark that should end the sentence. If there is no mistake, choose the letter D.

6 At what time did the train arrive.
   A  .
   B  ?
   C  !
   D  No mistake

7 I was so excited that I nearly jumped up and down.
   A  ?
   B  !
   C  ,
   D  No mistake

**8** Christopher Columbus set sail for India in 1492.

Ⓐ !
Ⓑ ?
Ⓒ ,
Ⓓ No mistake

**Directions:** Read the sentence with a blank. Choose the answer that fits best in the blank and has the correct punctuation and capitalization.

**9** We always enjoy going to _____.

Ⓐ Tim's house?
Ⓑ Tims' house.
Ⓒ Tim's house.
Ⓓ Tims" house.

**10** Have you seen the _____.

Ⓐ childrens' playground.
Ⓑ Childrens' playground?
Ⓒ children's playground.
Ⓓ children's playground?

**11** I _____ go out last night.

Ⓐ could'nt
Ⓑ couldn't
Ⓒ couldn't'

**12** I like to play ball with _____.

Ⓐ Tom, Dick, and Harry.
Ⓑ Tom Dick and Harry.
Ⓒ Tom, Dick, and Harry?

**13** Our pet cat had five cute little _____.

Ⓐ kittens'
Ⓑ kittens.
Ⓒ Kitten's.
Ⓓ Kittens?

(See page 101 for answer key.)

# CHAPTER 5

# Language Expression

Language expression covers what we think of as traditional grammar: identifying subject and predicate, using the correct form of a verb, and rewriting sentences in correct form. Writing topic sentences is also an important skill covered in fifth grade.

## Education Goals for Fifth Graders

Fifth graders should be comfortable with the basics of traditional grammar, be able to identify the subject and predicate of a sentence, and be able to rewrite sentences correctly.

Many school districts now require that each student write a five-paragraph essay containing topic sentences before the district will award a high school diploma. Therefore, any time you spend with your child on topic sentences in fifth grade will pay off in future years! In addition, speaking English without grammatical errors is a skill that opens doors in future careers.

## What You and Your Child Can Do

The most important strategy in the area of language expression is to model proper English and to correct poor English whenever you hear it used. Although I don't advocate spending much time watching TV on school nights, it's amazing how many grammatical errors you can hear on TV and radio.

By fifth grade, teachers expect that children can not only use the conversational, everyday language that we use in informal interactions, but that they can also use and understand the formal register, which is the language used in textbooks. This isn't formally taught, but children are expected to learn it by listening to formal speakers or by reading textbooks. It's one thing to understand this sentence:

My dog Millie has a very small pelvis.

It's much more difficult to understand the formal register:

Some breeds of dogs are prone to skeletal problems caused by overbreeding.

It may help to tell your child that if he wants to write and punctuate more formal sentences, he should pretend he is writing and talking like the newscasters on TV.

## What Tests May Ask

Your child will be expected to edit sentences for grammatical errors such as the wrong form of a verb, the wrong pronoun, or a subject and verb that do not agree. He will have to combine simple sentences to make a complex sentence and punctuate it correctly. He will have to find the best topic sentence for a paragraph, and he will probably have to edit a paragraph.

### Parts of Speech

Most children don't enjoy learning the parts of speech. It's true today and it's probably always been true. Names like "noun" and "predicate" (verb) just don't mean anything to a child. The idea that words can be sorted into categories and can change categories depending on the sentence is a pretty tough one to get across.

For example, the word *gossip* has two different functions in the following two sentences:

Our next-door neighbor was a terrible *gossip*.

The minister asked the congregation not to *gossip*.

In the first sentence, *gossip* is a noun; in the second sentence, it is a verb or predicate.

## What Your Fifth Grader Should Be Learning

Your child will have to identify the simple subjects and simple predicates of sentences. On some tests the child is expected to be able to identify a verb, a noun, an adjective, and an adverb.

## What You Can Do

Your fifth grader has the cognitive skills to learn parts of speech and to understand that words can change category, provided that teaching is on his level. The more concrete the approach, the better. It's also best to be sure the child can identify one part of speech well before you begin introducing others.

Try this technique: Make a chart to introduce the parts of speech. Buy a set of colored markers for each child. Begin with articles, which are the easiest, to introduce the activity. At the top of the chart, write the word *articles* in black marker and list the three articles:

the

a

an

Next, write some sentences in pen on notebook paper and let your fifth grader circle any articles he can find in the sentences. You could also tear out pages from a newspaper or magazine and let him find the articles. Have him say the word *article* as he circles the articles so that he memorizes the word through repetition.

The next day, introduce the idea of a noun (person, place, or thing). Nouns are underlined in blue. On the chart, write *nouns* in blue and write "person, place, or thing" beside it to help your child to remember. Let him find nouns and articles in any printed material you provide, underlining or circling them with the colored markers.

When your child can find nouns reliably, introduce verbs. Be sure he has completely mastered nouns and articles first, because children can easily become confused if you introduce too much too fast. Have your children give you six nouns while you are driving in the car (two people, two places, two things) or have them find three nouns in a sentence you make up. The reward might be a piece of candy—keep the glove compartment stocked!

The tricky part about verbs is that there are two kinds for you to put on your chart: action verbs and linking verbs. Use red marker for the verbs, and list action verbs as something that involves movement. Linking verbs are hard for children to understand, so list the most common ones on your chart: *is, are, was, were, have, had, appear.*

Finally, follow the same steps to teach the personal pronouns: *I, you, he, she, it, they, we, us, them, him,* and *her.* Use a yellow marker for this part of speech. Be sure your child is saying the name of the part of speech as he circles words.

These parts of speech are enough to identify the subjects and predicates that are covered on most exams. However, if your school district expects the student to master the other parts of speech, use green for prepositions. (The most common prepositions are *with, in, on,* and *for.*)

Purple is a good choice for adjectives, because adjectives modify nouns and most children can understand that blue and purple go together. Use orange for adverbs, which often modify verbs; again, red and orange seem to go together.

Now it's time to work on the subject of a sentence. Simply have the child find the noun that the subject is about. Or, have the child find the verb of the sentence and then ask: "Who did action in the verb?" Either way, your child will have located the noun that is acting as the subject of the sentence. When he finds the verb for the sentence, he will have located the predicate. If the child has to find the simple subject or the simple predicate, he must limit himself to one word, so tell him to find the most important word.

For instance:

Your Gortex parka is on the floor.

Actually, the entire subject is *your Gortex parka,* but *parka* is the simple subject. Using the colored markers, your child will quickly see that *is* is the only candidate for the position of predicate in that sentence.

Some parents have bought the refrigerator magnet sets of various words and let their children sort words into parts of speech categories. You can also play games in the car, like this one: "Give me a sentence in which *run* is used as a verb. Then give me a sentence in which *run* is used as a noun." This sort of activity can get pretty tedious, so use funny sentences to keep your child going. (Poking good-natured fun at siblings, teachers, principals, and parents is usually a winner with fifth graders!)

## Practice Skills: Parts of Speech

**Directions:** For each sentence, find the italicized word that is the simple subject of the sentence.

1   The *seagulls followed* the *ship* all the
       Ⓐ          Ⓑ                Ⓒ
   way to *Martha's Vineyard.*
            Ⓓ

2   The *scientists discovered* prehistoric
         Ⓐ          Ⓑ
   *fossils* in the African *valley.*
     Ⓒ                        Ⓓ

3   *Because* it was *cold, we* wore *gloves* and
     Ⓐ              Ⓑ Ⓒ          Ⓓ
   ski caps to school.

4   *Christopher Reeves* is an *inspiration* to
     Ⓐ                        Ⓑ
   many *disabled citizens.*
         Ⓒ        Ⓓ

**Directions:** For each sentence, find the simple predicate of the sentence.

5   The *children ran* gladly onto the
         Ⓐ      Ⓑ
   playground, *shouting* and *laughing.*
                Ⓒ              Ⓓ

6   Our new *computer has* a wonderful
              Ⓐ      Ⓑ
   *graphics program.*
     Ⓒ        Ⓓ

7   My *family* in *Oregon traveled* to Mount
         Ⓐ        Ⓑ      Ⓒ
   Hood for a *skiing* trip.
                Ⓓ

8   My *grandparents lived* in a *rambling*
         Ⓐ          Ⓑ          Ⓒ
   Victorian *three-story* house.
              Ⓓ

(See page 101 for answer key.)

## Correct Usage

## What Your Fifth Grader Should Be Learning

Your child will be expected to choose correct standard English sentences, and to correctly use present, past, and future verb tenses. He will have to combine sentences to form new complex or compound sentences.

## What You Can Do

The best way to improve standard English is to use it yourself and to correct your children when they make a mistake:

Not *me and Bill,* dear. Say *Bill and I.*

Don't say, *They should clean up the mess their-selves.* Say, *They should clean it up themselves.*

If you notice that your child is making grammatical errors in his homework, use those sentences as examples to correct. If you're having trouble making up sentences, look for an old grammar textbook from the 1950s or 1960s. There are many sentences to correct, and kids usually get a kick out of the sentences that seem so dated to them. Do a few sentences each night after dinner.

If your children can read in the car without getting carsick, have them read out the sentences from the old grammar book. Everyone can take a turn correctly reading them out loud in return for a piece of the hard candy in your pocket.

Your child will also be expected to combine simple sentences into a correctly punctuated complex sentence. This is an important skill, because children are expected to use a variety of sentence types when they write essays in high school and college. One easy way to combine sentences is to cross out any words that appear more than once and then combine the remaining words into a reasonable sentence:

Mrs. Jones is our cafeteria manager.

Mrs. Jones makes delicious banana pudding.

Your child will need to use commas correctly to make the complex sentence:

Mrs. Jones, our cafeteria manager, makes delicious banana pudding.

## Practice Skills: Correct Usage

**Directions:** Choose the correct form of the verb.

9   Next week our Boy Scout troop _____ up Springer Mountain.
   Ⓐ   hike
   Ⓑ   hiking
   Ⓒ   is hiking
   Ⓓ   will hike

10   I was so thirsty after the race that I _____ an entire quart of water.
   Ⓐ   drink
   Ⓑ   drank
   Ⓒ   will drink
   Ⓓ   have drunk

11   In the last game, our pitcher _____ a perfect game.
   Ⓐ   is throwing
   Ⓑ   throws
   Ⓒ   will throw
   Ⓓ   threw

12   Bill always _____ a walking stick when he hikes.
   Ⓐ   take
   Ⓑ   takes
   Ⓒ   took
   Ⓓ   is taking

**Directions:** Choose the answer that best combines the underlined sentences.

13  The car has a dead battery.

   The car is on the side of the road.

   (A)  The car has a dead battery, and the car is on the side of the road.

   (B)  On the side of the road is the car with the dead battery.

   (C)  With a dead battery, the car was left on the side of the road.

   (D)  The car on the side of the road has a dead battery.

14  My new dress is blue.

   My new dress has a short skirt.

   My new dress has short sleeves.

   (A)  My new blue dress has a short skirt and short sleeves.

   (B)  My new dress is blue, having a short skirt and sleeves.

   (C)  I have a new dress which is blue, short-sleeved, and short-skirted.

   (D)  My new dress is blue and it has short sleeves and it has a short skirt.

(See page 101 for answer key.)

## Topic Sentences

The final skill typically covered in language expression on most achievement tests is writing topic sentences. Children often find topic sentences difficult to formulate; they may not understand that the topic sentence is the sentence that expresses the main point of the paragraph.

## What Your Fifth Grader Should Be Learning

Fifth graders are expected to be able to identify the topic sentence and to understand that it expresses the main point of the paragraph.

## What You Can Do

Finding the topic sentence is easily done in a nonfiction book or in a textbook. Begin by pointing out the topic sentence to the child when you are doing homework with him or reading aloud at night. Then let your child find the topic sentence for himself when he's reading in his science or social studies book. Because he'll only have to recognize the topic sentence on most standardized tests at this point, you can stop with simple recognition. However, it's a good idea to be sure your child can write a simple topic sentence when he has to write an essay or paragraph for school.

The topic sentence is usually the first sentence in a paragraph. If the first sentence is designed to create interest, the topic sentence may be located at the end of the first introductory paragraph.

Before letting your child write a word of the paragraph, have him talk about the ideas he will include. You can jot them down. Then let him decide which points or ideas he'll include. Finally, have him write a sentence that tells the point of his paragraph.

When the sentence is well-formed and to the point, have him write it down and then begin his essay. It's much easier to write a good paragraph when some thinking and oral discussion are done first.

## What Tests May Ask

On most standardized tests, the child won't have to write the topic sentence; he'll simply have to recognize it from a set of examples. This is a lot easier than writing his own topic sentences. He simply has to ask himself: "Is this sentence the main point of this paragraph? Is it related to every other sentence in the paragraph?" If the answer to both questions is "yes," he has found the topic sentence.

## Practice Skills: Topic Sentences

**Directions:** Read the paragraph below. Find the best topic sentence for the paragraph.

**15** _____. There are jet airplanes that carry passengers across the country or across an ocean in a few hours. There are hot air balloons that take small groups aloft by relying on heated air and wind currents. There are helicopters that track traffic patterns in large metro areas. There are reconnaissance planes that gather information while hurtling around the world at speeds faster than the speed of sound. There are even space shuttles that have flown missions to space stations orbiting around the world.

(A) There are many kinds of planes.

(B) There are powered and unpowered aircraft.

(C) The skies overhead are filled with many different types of aircraft.

**16** _____. You should fertilize plants on a regular basis so that the plant has a good supply of nutrients to encourage strong growth. You should prune the plants carefully so that air can circulate around the plants and discourage the spread of disease. You should also be sure that the soil around the plants is well-drained so that parasites can't easily grow in the overly moist soil.

(A) It is easy to be a good gardener.

(B) Taking good care of your plants is the best way to discourage disease.

(C) Parasites grow where it is wet.

(D) You need to fertilize your plants if they are going to grow to be strong.

(See page 101 for answer key.)

# CHAPTER 6

# Spelling and Study Skills

Spelling is a controversial subject these days. Many people feel that spell-checkers have made the study of spelling obsolete, and that students have so much else to learn that spelling should be low on the list of priorities.

However, most teachers believe there's still a need for correct spelling of common words. There are many occasions when we have to write, and spelling errors can be embarrassing. In addition, many school districts that have established high-stakes testing count spelling errors against the student's total score. If you live in such a district, you need to emphasize spelling with your child.

## Education Goals for Fifth Graders

Some researchers believe spelling is almost an inborn skill; for these students, spelling takes almost no effort. After one or two exposures to a word, these kids can memorize the letters in order and they don't forget the word the day after the test. On the other hand, some students seem almost unable to spell no matter what they do. Even after drilling the words all week, they may not be able to spell correctly on the test; and if they manage the test on Friday, they've forgotten how to spell the words by Monday.

## What Tests May Ask

This chapter includes some helpful techniques to use for children who seem to be naturally poor spellers, since standardized tests still ask spelling questions. Tests also assess study skills, including map reading, outlines, and use of a dictionary, glossary, index, and table of contents.

## Spelling

### What Your Fifth Grader Should Be Learning

By fifth grade, your child should be able to spell the 1,000 most frequently used words in English. There are many published lists of these words; one of the best-known is called the Rebecca Sitton Word List.

In addition, fifth graders should be able to edit their own compositions for misspelled words on a computer or by using a dictionary.

A spelling dictionary may be especially helpful. This is a list of words without meanings in which words with the same root are listed together, such as *sob, sobbed,* and *sobbing.* This type of research tool is a lot easier for children to use than a large dictionary.

Finally, children should know some spelling rules of English: that we double the final consonant before adding *-ing;* that *i* comes before *e* except after the letter *c;* and that the final consonant is doubled before adding *y,* but not before adding *ey.*

## What You Can Do

Most parents have developed a routine for spelling with their children by fifth grade. Some parents simply call out the words and have the child spell the word out loud. Others insist that the child write the words until they are memorized. Some parents use a combination of methods. If these methods are working for you, skip the next section.

**Analyze Errors.** If your child doesn't spell easily, you may find that the traditional methods don't work. In this case, look at your child's spelling tests for the last few weeks. If she can spell the words on the test, but misspells them the week after in her writing, analyze her errors. She may be an inventive speller, who spells the word exactly as it sounds: *nodee* for the word *naughty*. Or perhaps she tries to spell the word as it looks but makes errors of omission (*wistle*) or errors of sequence (*whistel*).

**Emphasize Spelling Patterns.** Children who make these kinds of mistakes need more study of English spelling patterns. While many people stress the irregular spellings of English words (like *through* or *know*), most English words fall into regular patterns. Helping your child to recognize the patterns should improve her spelling.

If your child is a poor speller, it's best if the spelling program doesn't consist of words taken from the stories being read in language arts that week. Spelling words should be grouped by spelling patterns, not by meaning. Poor spellers need frequent exposure to spelling patterns and they need to be told explicitly about the patterns they will find in words. Don't expect a poor speller to notice that *fudge, wedge,* and *lodge* all have a *d* that you can hardly hear when the word is spoken. If they noticed these things on their own, they would be good spellers!

**Use Memory Aids.** There are many different ways to help fifth graders memorize, and you'll need to find the way that works best for your child. If your child is a poor speller, ask the teacher to send home the spelling list on Friday instead of waiting until Monday. Then you can begin the words on Sunday to give your child an extra day of practice. Many children simply

need repeated practice sessions to get the words right. You can call words at night after supper or you can do it in the car on the way to piano lessons.

When you get the list, scan the words to see if there are any easy words that your child may already know or that she could easily figure out. Practice these only a few times. Turn your attention to words that your child doesn't know and that appear difficult, and try to come up with some memory tricks to help with these harder words:

- *Shapes:* Does the word have an unusual shape that would help the child to spell it? The word *style* has a short letter, then a tall letter, then a letter with a tail, then a tall letter, and then a short letter.

- *Pattern:* Is there a common spelling pattern that you have learned previously? If your child can spell *apple* she can spell *hobble*.

- *Sound:* Can you think of a way to pronounce the word that would make the spelling easier? For instance, say *fry-end* for *friend*.

- *Sing:* Can you spell the word aloud in a singsong tone or even in a melody? For example, sing the spelling of *success* to the melody of *Twinkle, Twinkle, Little Star.*

- *Cheer:* Can you make the spelling into a cheer that you repeat 10 times? Try shouting "o-f-f-e-r" 10 times with your child.

**Keep Practicing.** After the spelling test is over and your child has done well, don't forget those words in your haste to move on to the new list. Keep an index card in your purse with a list of words that were particularly hard for your child to learn. Only include words that you think your child will need in her writing, words like *night, through,* and *measure.* Exclude words like *rhinoceros* or *receipt.*

Practice these words at odd times during the day, such as when you're in the car. Ask your child to spell a word that she knew a week or two ago, and give a reward for good performance (for example, five correct spellings earn one night without having to unload the dishwasher).

---

**IF ALL ELSE FAILS**...

If you come to a word that just doesn't lend itself to any of these methods, there is one method reserved for the hardest-to-teach spelling words. Buy various squares of material from the remnant bins at the fabric store (corduroy and velvet seem to work best). Have the child place the material over her thigh and spell the word aloud with you while tracing the word with her pointer finger. Have her repeat the finger spelling until she can do it with her eyes closed. It's amazing that a tactile approach can work so well—but you must use it sparingly!

---

## Practice Skills: Spelling

**Directions:** Read each word and choose the word that has a spelling error. If there is no mistake, select the last choice.

1.  (A) population
    (B) explotion
    (C) peace
    (D) regular
    (E) no mistakes

2.  (A) television
    (B) offered
    (C) decision
    (D) lately
    (E) no mistakes

3.  (A) journal
    (B) grabbed
    (C) intrest
    (D) expression
    (E) no mistakes

4.  (A) ceiling
    (B) breakfast
    (C) declaration
    (D) composion
    (E) no mistakes

---

**Directions:** Find the word that is spelled correctly and that will fit into the blank.

5.  A birthday is a special _____.
    (A) accasion
    (B) occasion
    (C) occasson
    (D) ocasion

6.  My mother loves to direct the _____.
    (A) chair
    (B) quire
    (C) choir
    (D) chore

7.  We used to call the "media center" a _____.
    (A) liberry
    (B) library
    (C) libarry
    (D) librare

8.  Camels are able to survive the harsh conditions of the _____.
    (A) dessert
    (B) desart
    (C) disert
    (D) desert

(See page 101 for answer key.)

## Study Skills

## What Your Fifth Grader Should Be Learning

Your fifth grader should be able to use her dictionary with ease, using guide words to locate the entries, determining what part of speech the word is, understanding that multiple listings may be given, and figuring out the pronunciation of the word. She should also be able to identify and use the features of her textbooks—the table of contents, the glossary, the index, and the appendix—to locate information. She should be able to glean information from maps and outlines.

## What You Can Do

There are usually not many items in this section of the test, so you do not need to emphasize it as much as other areas. Your child probably has to use a dictionary and glossary in her homework assignments, especially in science, social studies, and spelling.

One evening when you're going over material for the next social studies test, ask your child what the index and appendix are used for in her text. See if she can use the table of contents quickly and accurately. You will probably have noticed some of the maps in her books; see if she can locate information on some of the maps. Most children will have had lots of practice in these basic skills by fifth grade in order to answer basic study skills questions.

## Practice Skills: Study Skills

**Directions:** Read each question and mark the correct answer.

Look at these guide words from a dictionary page.

### CRAB – CUTE

9 Which word will be found on the page?
- (A) cranberry
- (B) cuticle
- (C) cane
- (D) candle

Look at these guide words from a dictionary page.

### STRAIGHT – STRUM

10 Which word will be found on the page?
- (A) stitch
- (B) scheme
- (C) style
- (D) strict

**Directions:** Study the map below and answer the following questions.

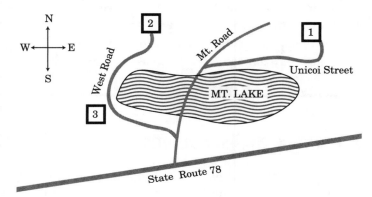

KEY:  1. Lodge  2. General Store  3. Camping Area

11 What state road would you have to travel on to reach the recreation area?
- (A) Mountain Road
- (B) Unicoi Street
- (C) West Road
- (D) Route 78

12 If you were walking on Mountain Road, crossing the lake and heading toward Unicoi Street, in what direction would you be walking?
- (A) north
- (B) east
- (C) west
- (D) south

**13** On what street is the General Store located?

- Ⓐ State Route 78
- Ⓑ Unicoi Street
- Ⓒ Mountain Road
- Ⓓ West Road

**14** Which of the following is a physical feature on the map?

- Ⓐ the General Store
- Ⓑ the Lodge
- Ⓒ Mountain Lake
- Ⓓ State Route 78

**Directions:** Study the title page below and answer the following questions.

# The Mighty Chicken

### Henry W. Talbott

Poultry Books        New York

1999

**15** What is the title of this book?

- Ⓐ Poultry Books
- Ⓑ Henry W. Talbott
- Ⓒ New York
- Ⓓ The Mighty Chicken

**16** What does the year 1999 indicate?

- Ⓐ The year the book was written
- Ⓑ The year the book was published
- Ⓒ The year the author was born

**Directions:** Study the dictionary entry below and answer the following questions.

> **plan** *n.* 1. a scheme, method, or design to obtain some object. 2. a sketch, drawing, or draft of an object such as a building.
>
> **planned, planning** *v.* 1. To form a method for obtaining some object. 2. To design or make a sketch of a building. <L *planum* level ground <*planus*

**17** What part of speech is the word *plan*?

- Ⓐ noun
- Ⓑ verb
- Ⓒ adjective
- Ⓓ noun and verb

**18** From what language did we get the word *plan*?

- Ⓐ French
- Ⓑ Greek
- Ⓒ Spanish
- Ⓓ Latin

**19** What spelling rule applies to the word *plan*?

- Ⓐ A silent *e* on the end makes the vowel long.
- Ⓑ Double the final consonant before adding *-ing* or *-ed*.
- Ⓒ The vowel *i* usually comes before *e* except after *c*.

**20** Which meaning of the word *plan* is used in this sentence?

**The architect brought the *plans* for our new home.**

- Ⓐ first verb meaning
- Ⓑ first noun meaning
- Ⓒ second verb meaning
- Ⓓ second noun meaning

**21** Which meaning of the word *plan* is used in this sentence?

**The football coach *planned* a new passing play to win the game.**

- Ⓐ first noun meaning
- Ⓑ first verb meaning
- Ⓒ second noun meaning
- Ⓓ second verb meaning

(See page 101 for answer key.)

# CHAPTER 7

# Math Concepts

Math concepts represent a difficult area for many students as well as for their parents. This area includes several types of skills, including numeration (reading or naming numbers) and number concepts (place value, even numbers, odd numbers, multiples, Roman numerals, and prime numbers).

## Education Goals for Fifth Graders

Math concepts for fifth graders include a wide range of skills from place value and prime numbers to long division and geometry, many of which may seem foreign to you. Of all the subjects studied in school today, mathematics is the one course that most often entails homework (usually nightly). It takes a lot of practice to learn the complex processes needed to do long division or multiply like denominators.

## What You and Your Child Can Do

Daily homework can be a gift for a parent whose child is weak in math. You'll have a daily window into your child's classroom, and you'll be able to find out what the teacher has taught that day. You'll also be able to determine whether your child has mastered the process or needs more practice. Look through the fifth-grade math book while your child is doing something else to see exactly what he's responsible for learning. Notice how the concept is presented; this is crucial.

You may have vivid memories of your own school days, when you just didn't understand what your teacher presented in math. That night, the homework might as well have been the hieroglyphics inscribed on the Rosetta Stone. Luckily, you had a parent who was good in math, and Mom or Dad did remember how to do the problem. Hallelujah! But when Dad or Mom launched into the explanation, it sounded nothing like the teacher's presentation! Of course, you shut down right then and there, as any self-respecting child would do. It was the teacher's way or none at all!

Remembering this awful episode, you can see that you really must try to learn the way that your child is being taught math. There are usually many different ways to solve math problems, but you'll do best if you find the method your child's math book prefers and stick to that. Math is hard enough to learn without adding confusion at this point.

After your child has learned one method well, he can find out that there are other ways to do things. Let that understanding wait for another day. For this particular type of math, it's not a good idea to invent your own games for the car or the dinner table. Instead, stick closely to your child's math book.

If you can't figure out the process, call the teacher. Most teachers are only too happy to support your efforts to work with your child on an area of weakness. Don't be embarrassed to admit you've forgotten the process, learned it a different way, or never knew it to begin with. Your child's teacher was once in fifth grade too.

## Contacting the Teacher

The attitude you convey when you talk to your child's teacher is all-important. Put yourself in her shoes. She's expected to cover a large amount of material with a group of children who are working on many different levels. She may have students in her class with a variety of barriers to learning, many of which are totally beyond her control. She knows that her job is to teach, but she also has to convey discipline, respect, time management, and a multitude of other values. And she has 25 to 50 parents to manage, not to mention a school full of adults (her colleagues, the principal, the custodian, the school nurse, and the school secretary) to deal with. It's a tough job, it doesn't pay very well, and it's physically and emotionally exhausting. When you call the teacher with a problem, let her know that you're not criticizing her. Let her know that you're both on the same team: the team of adults who care about your child. Treat her as a competent professional and ask for her help and advice. After all, she sees a side of your child that you don't see. Most teachers are thrilled when parents are willing to reinforce what they're teaching, so build a good partnership. It will pay off richly.

One more suggestion: Think of how great you feel when the teacher says something lovely about your child. Try sending the teacher a nice note when you appreciate something she did. If your child comes home enthused about a unit on the Statue of Liberty, write a note saying that you heard about it at the supper table and that you appreciate her efforts. She'll probably save that note in a special file that all teachers have, the file of notes they read on days when they wonder why they ever decided to be teachers.

## Math Phobia

Around fifth grade, many students (but especially girls) develop a fear or dislike of math. This is unfortunate, because many of the best-paying professions require excellence in math: accountants, architects, engineers, financial officers, physicians, scientists, management information specialists. It's a shame that our sons and daughters can fall off the career train early in their lives just because they don't understand how to think mathematically. Many students are blocked from honors diplomas or college preparatory diplomas because their math skills are not well developed by eighth grade.

If you sense that your child is struggling with math, now is the time to concentrate on helping him to develop the skills and vocabulary to do well. If you notice that your daughter is developing math phobia, be sure to give her the help she needs to feel comfortable. Math is not a man's field.

# What Tests May Ask

Your child can expect to find plenty of questions about math concepts on most standardized tests, including reading or naming numbers, place value, even numbers, odd numbers, multiples, Roman numerals, and prime numbers. If you notice that your child is weak in these areas and you decide to help, you'll have to learn some new math concepts as well.

## Numeration

Numeration simply means reading or naming numbers. In first grade, your child learned that the funny little squiggle with the two half-circles was called a three and meant three things. By fifth grade, your child has a far more sophisticated concept of numbers.

# What Your Fifth Grader Should Be Learning

A fifth grader should be able to locate high numbers on a number line and understand that the number 36 means a number with 3 tens and 6 ones. By now, he can use his cognitive flexibility to know that 36 can also be written as 2 tens and 16 ones. He probably knows all the ordinals, which are first, second, third, and so on.

This year, he'll learn some new math words to help him name numbers in new ways. For example, he'll learn terms like factor, greatest common factor, common multiples, exponent, and square root.

Many parents are shocked to see words like exponent and square root in a fifth-grade math book, but our push for higher standards has led textbook authors to introduce these concepts earlier and earlier. However, these concepts aren't taught in great depth. A child should simply be able to compute an easy exponent, like $10^2 = 100$. He should also know that the square root of 25 is 5 and recognize the radical symbol $(\sqrt{})$. Finally, he should be able to solve an expanded numeration, which means writing a number like 1245 like this:

$$(1 \times 1000) + (2 \times 100) + (4 \times 10) + (5 \times 1)$$

## What You Can Do

Probably the easiest thing to do is check your child's math homework and math papers that come home daily or on Friday. Determine whether your child is having trouble with any of the skills discussed above. You might simply quiz your child one weekend on the problems that follow this section. But give a *big* bonus for doing math on the weekend, especially math that wasn't assigned by the teacher! Once you have identified the area of weakness, you can take a logical approach to see where the problem lies.

The most likely explanation is that your child just doesn't remember or understand the math vocabulary. After all, greatest common factor or least common denominator are pretty scary-sounding terms.

If this is the case, you need to teach this vocabulary. Remember: The poor teacher goes to

where the child should be and calls him to come to her. The good teacher goes to where the child is and walks him over to where he should be. Let's say that you're trying to teach the term *greatest common factor:*

PARENT: Honey, I'm getting the idea that you don't know what a *greatest common factor* is.

CHILD: Well, Mrs. Rigsby keeps on talking about it but I just don't know what she is saying up there and I can't do the problems on the board like the other kids. I'm scared that she'll call on me and then the other guys will see…

PARENT: Okay, Okay, I get the picture. Well, let's break this math word apart. You know what the word *greatest* means, right?

CHILD: Geez, I'm not that stupid!

PARENT: No offense intended. I'm just trying to see exactly where you are coming from. So you know the first word. How about *common*? Does that word mean anything to you?

CHILD: Well, not really.

PARENT: Okay, what if I asked you what you and your brother have in common?

CHILD: Not much! If he messes up my video games one more time…

PARENT: So tell me what common means, if you have nothing in common with your brother.

CHILD: Well, it means what do you have that is alike, what do you share, what do you have that's the same. Like that jerk and I have our parents in common and that is about it. We share the same parents and that's all.

PARENT: Good example. Now in this problem, Mrs. Rigsby wants you to find the greatest common factors of 12 and 18. We'll use your example about your brother in a minute, but first, do you know what a factor is?

CHILD: Yeah, sort of. Like 25 has three factors, 1, 5, and 25.

PARENT: How did you figure that out?

CHILD: You just have to go through your times

tables and think of all the facts that might equal 25. 25 is either 5 times 5 or 1 times 25, so the factors are 1, 5, and 25.

PARENT: Good. You are right on the verge of understanding this greatest common factor problem.

CHILD: I am? I think you must be dreaming.

PARENT: No, just listen. Pretend that 25 is a child with four parents. Now in the land of numbers, children can have any number of parents, not like human children who can only have two birth parents. 25 has four parents; 25 and 1 and also 5 and 5. Now what about the number 18? Who are 18's parents?

CHILD: Well, he would have 1 and 18, 2 and 9, and 3 and 6. Geez, he has six parents to get on his nerves and make him do chores.

PARENT: I am going to write out those six parents. Now what parents does 12 have?

CHILD: Well, he has 1 and 12, 2 and 6, 3 and 4, and that's all.

PARENT: Now I have written out 12's parents underneath 18's parents. Why don't you take my pencil and cross out any parents these two numbers don't have in common.

CHILD: Well, I would have to cross out 12, 18, and 9. They have 1, 2, 3, and 6 in common.

PARENT: Now how about if we use the word *factor* instead of *parent*? It sounds much fancier anyway. Of the four common parents (or factors) you have left over, which number is the greatest one—the greatest common factor?

CHILD: Now I see! It's 6. Geez, why didn't she just tell me how to do this? This is simple!

Very often you will find that "difficulty with math" is really "difficulty with vocabulary." Always check the vocabulary first and, if necessary, break the term down into words that your child can identify with. Don't be afraid to be silly, like telling your child that a number has parents. Some of the silliest memory clues are the best because a child remembers them, all

the while complaining about how dumb the memory aid is.

There is a second problem that might underlie your child's weakness in math concepts. Does he really know his math facts? The child in the example above instantly knew that 25 has only two multiplication facts to its name: $1 \times 25$ and $5 \times 5$. If your child doesn't know the times tables, you could explain the problem above using a card on which all the times tables are printed. In fact, if your child knows some of the facts but not all, you probably should use a card to be sure that your child identifies all the factors. But there is no substitute for knowing all the math facts quickly and accurately. This will be discussed in detail in Chapter 8.

## Practice Skills: Numeration

**Directions:** Read each problem and choose the correct answer.

**1** 36 =
- (A) $5^2$
- (B) $6^2$
- (C) $10^2$
- (D) $1^2$

---

**2** Your mother is in line at the drive-through to get you a hamburger. She is fifth in line. How many cars are ahead of you?
- (A) 6
- (B) 3
- (C) 4
- (D) 1

---

**3** What number is expressed by:

$$(6 \times 1000) + (6 \times 100) + (0 \times 10) + (6 \times 1)$$

- (A) 6,066
- (B) 6,666
- (C) 6,600
- (D) 6,606

---

## Practice Skills: Number Concepts

**Directions:** Read each problem and choose the correct answer.

**11** What is another name for the Roman numeral XIII?

(A) 13    (B) 8
(C) 53    (D) 3

**12** What rule can you use to find the number that is missing from the pattern below?

| 3 | 9 | 10 | 30 | 31 | 93 | 94 |

(A) Multiply each number by 3.
(B) Multiply each number by 13.
(C) Add 1 to each number.
(D) Multiply one number by 3. For the next number add 1.

**13** 636,550 =

(A) Six hundred thirty-six thousand, five hundred and fifty thousandths.
(B) Six hundred thirty-six thousand, five hundred and fifty.
(C) Six hundred thirty-six thousand, five hundred and fifty thousand.
(D) Six hundred thirty-seven thousand, five hundred and fifty.

**14** Which of these statements is true about the numbers in the box?

| 3 | 7 | 11 | 19 | 23 |

(A) They are all odd numbers.
(B) They are all even numbers.
(C) They are all odd numbers and also all prime numbers.
(D) They are all prime numbers.

**15** Which of these numbers is both even and a multiple of 7?

(A) 36    (B) 49
(C) 56    (D) 63

**16** What does the 6 in 269,114 mean?

(A) 6       (B) 60
(C) 6000    (D) 60,000

**17** In which of these numerals does 2 have the greatest value?

(A) 20,617    (B) 42,918
(C) 2467      (D) 14,562

**18** How much would the value of 87,244 be increased by replacing the 7 with a 9?

(A) 200     (B) 2000
(C) 3000    (D) 5000

**19** Which statement about place value is true?

(A) 10 hundreds are equal to 1000
(B) 10 hundreds are equal to 10,000.
(C) 10 hundreds are equal to 100,000.
(D) 10 hundreds are equal to 1,000,000.

**20** These squares show groups of numbers that are related by the same rule. Figure out the rule and then choose the number that is missing from the second square.

| 18 | 27 |
| 2 | 3 |

| 45 | 54 |
| ? | 6 |

| 108 | 81 |
| 12 | 9 |

(A) 7    (B) a
(C) 5    (D) 8

(See pages 101–102 for answer key.)

## Number Properties

The term *number properties* sounds unfamiliar to most adults, but there are just three main skills tested in this area:

- rounding or estimation;
- the use of number sentences; and
- the order in which operations are done to solve a simple equation.

## What Your Fifth Grader Should Be Learning

Your child has been rounding and estimating since first grade. Now, in fifth grade, he has to work at a more advanced level. He's probably familiar with number sentences, which are simple equations that contain only numbers, not alphabet letters representing variables. Operations refers to the four processes of addition, subtraction, multiplication, and division; but number operations problems may include exponents and parentheses.

## What You Can Do

It's probably unnecessary to spend much time on the process of estimation. In fact, this is one skill you can work on without the math book. Adults estimate all the time: "It'll just take me five minutes to get this roast in the oven." "I've got about an acre of grass to fertilize, so I'll need the family-size bag of lawn food."

Be sure to look for examples of estimation in your daily life—when cooking, shopping, or estimating the time it takes to do something. Let your child help you out with these examples and he'll become a good estimator.

Number sentences aren't so tough either. Typically, the child will have to decide whether a number sentence is true or false. He may have to substitute numbers into missing number boxes to come up with a true math sentence, or he may be asked to put the correct sign for one of the four operations into a box to make a sen-

tence true. If he knows number facts, he'll be able to do this, especially if you've been working on the inductive reasoning discussed earlier.

Solving number sentences that contain more than one kind of operation is easy too, if your child knows the secret clue: *Please Excuse My Dear Aunt Sally.* This memory aid gives the order of operations to perform:

1. Do anything inside of **P**arentheses.
2. Do anything related to **E**xponents.
3. **M**ultiply.
4. **D**ivide.
5. **A**dd.
6. **S**ubtract.

There is one more notation that might confuse you, but is probably old news to your fifth grader. The symbols < and > stand for "less than" and "greater than." Your child probably learned in first grade that the symbol is an alligator's mouth and that the mouth always goes after the bigger number because the alligator is hungry. Thus $6 > 3$ but $2 < 5$.

## Practice Skills: Number Properties

**Directions:** Read each problem and choose the correct answer.

**21** The sum of 399 and 420 is closest to:

- (A) 900
- (B) 800
- (C) 700
- (D) 600

**22** Which number sentence is incorrect?

- (A) $5 + 0 = 5$
- (B) $5 - 0 = 5$
- (C) $0 \times 5 = 0$
- (D) $0 \times 5 = 5$

**23** Another name for 50 × 1000 is:

   Ⓐ  500 × 100
   Ⓑ  50 × 100
   Ⓒ  5000 × 100
   Ⓓ  50,000 × 100

**24** The owner of a bicycle factory receives an order for 150 racing bikes. Which number sentence shows how to find the total number of wheels the factory owner must order?

   Ⓐ  150 ÷ 2 = ☐
   Ⓑ  150 × 2 = ☐
   Ⓒ  150 + 2 = ☐
   Ⓓ  150 − 2 = ☐

**25** What is 678,944 rounded to the nearest hundred thousand?

   Ⓐ  600,000    Ⓑ  800,000
   Ⓒ  700,000    Ⓓ  900,000

**26** Which of these is the best estimate of 99 × 102?

   Ⓐ  100 × 110
   Ⓑ  100 × 120
   Ⓒ  90 × 100
   Ⓓ  100 × 100

**27** Which statement is true about this number sentence?

$$5237 ÷ 1000 = ☐$$

   Ⓐ  ☐ is greater than 6.
   Ⓑ  ☐ is less than 5.
   Ⓒ  ☐ is between 5 and 6.
   Ⓓ  ☐ is equal to 5.

**28** What symbol should replace the box in the number sentence below?

$$28 ÷ 4 \;☐\; 14 − 7$$

   Ⓐ  =       Ⓑ  +
   Ⓒ  −       Ⓓ  ×

(See pages 101–102 for answer key.)

## Fractions and Decimals

If there is one skill area that best characterizes fifth grade, it's the study of decimals and fractions.

# What Your Fifth Grader Should Be Learning

Fifth grade is the year to learn:

- what decimals and fractions are;
- changing fractions into decimals and decimals into fractions;
- adding, subtracting, multiplying, and dividing fractions and decimals;
- ordering fractions and decimals from smallest to largest; and
- finding the least common denominator.

These topics are difficult for students because they're working with abstract concepts and with processes that have several steps. But learning skills like this is good preparation for the worlds of algebra, geometry, and calculus, so encourage your child to persevere.

# What You Can Do

Most children get their first introduction to the world of fractions from the pie that is being constantly sliced into pieces of equal size. This is fine, because it is a concrete way to represent the fraction. But forget about pies when you have to multiply using fractions, because as your child knows, you can't multiply slices of pie!

Familiarity with commonly used fractions is a good thing. You can use your measuring spoons and measuring cups, as well as the markings on a ruler. To become familiar with decimals, use pennies and dimes as parts of a dollar. The main idea is that fractions and decimals both represent precise parts of a whole object, like a dollar.

Next, be sure your child is familiar with the math vocabulary of this part of the math world. Does he know a numerator from a denominator? Here's a way to help remember: The **d**enominator is always **d**own, and the *n* in *numerator* is the reverse of the *u* in *up*.

Does your child know how to find the least common denominator? Pay attention to the way your child's teacher is presenting this information. If you have to practice this skill with your child, use her method exactly.

When it comes to ordering fractions and decimals from least to greatest, you might want to use manipulatives so that your child sees for himself how this works. Once he has seen the actual ordering, he'll remember it much more easily than if you try to get him to memorize something abstract. For example, make your child a grid with six boxes across and two boxes down, for a total of twelve boxes. Let him color in one box and write $\frac{1}{12}$. Then color in two boxes and write $\frac{2}{12}$. It is easy to see that the larger the numerator, the larger the fraction. You can do the same thing for denominators; just make different-sized boxes to color. If you have two boxes and color one of them, that represents $\frac{1}{2}$. If you have three boxes and color one of them, you have $\frac{1}{3}$. As you continue, you see that the fractions decrease in size as the denominator increases. You can do the same thing with decimals using pennies ( .55 is certainly larger than .11).

The last obstacle is to convince your child that fractions and decimals are really just two different ways of saying the same thing: $\frac{1}{2}$ is the same as .5. You can show this by shading colored boxes, counting out pennies, and finally having your child divide the denominator into the numerator. No matter what he does, he will come out with the same answer.

## Practice Skills: Decimals and Fractions

**Directions:** Read each problem and choose the correct answer.

**29** Which group of decimals is ordered from least to greatest?

Ⓐ 4.123, 4.223, 4.323, 4.423
Ⓑ 4.423, 4.323, 4.223, 4.123
Ⓒ 4.423, 4.123, 4.567, 4.423
Ⓓ 4.423, 4.823, 4.023, 4.123

**30** Which of these fractions has a value that is less than $\frac{1}{5}$?

Ⓐ $\frac{1}{2}$      Ⓑ $\frac{1}{3}$
Ⓒ $\frac{2}{4}$      Ⓓ $\frac{1}{6}$

**31** How should you write twenty-one hundredths as a decimal?

Ⓐ 21.00      Ⓑ 2.100
Ⓒ 0.21      Ⓓ 0.021

**32** Which of these is between 0.14 and 0.22 in value?

Ⓐ 0.13      Ⓑ 0.19
Ⓒ 0.23      Ⓓ 0.01

**33** Which of these is another way to write $\frac{1}{6}$?

Ⓐ $\frac{2}{3}$      Ⓑ $\frac{1}{12}$
Ⓒ $\frac{2}{12}$      Ⓓ $\frac{6}{1}$

**34** What is the least common denominator of $\frac{1}{2}$, $\frac{1}{3}$, and $\frac{1}{6}$?

Ⓐ 6      Ⓑ 12
Ⓒ 24      Ⓓ 2

**35** What number belongs in the second denominator?

$$\frac{1}{4} = \frac{2}{\square}$$

Ⓐ 2      Ⓑ 4
Ⓒ 16      Ⓓ 8

**36** What decimal tells how much of this shape is shaded?

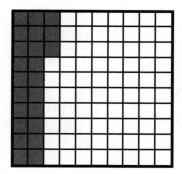

   Ⓐ   0.23
   Ⓑ   0.25
   Ⓒ   0.29
   Ⓓ   0.30

(See pages 101–102 for answer key.)

# CHAPTER 8

# Math Computation

**S**uccess on the computation portion of a standardized test depends on two skills: knowledge of the math facts and familiarity with the processes of regrouping, short division, long division, and operating with fractions. The basis of good computation is lightning-fast, automatic recall of the math facts for addition, subtraction, multiplication, and division.

## Education Goals for Fifth Graders

The math facts should be so well learned by fifth grade that your child hardly has to pause before stating the answer. When long division and multiplying with 2- or 3-digit multipliers must be done, your child can concentrate on the process instead of trying to remember math facts.

By this time, fifth graders should be on automatic pilot when regrouping (what you used to call borrowing and carrying). Fifth graders should be able to:

- Remember the four steps of a long division problem without confusion.

- Divide with remainders.

- Add and subtract fractions with like and unlike denominators.

## What You and Your Child Can Do

All second graders should know the addition and subtraction facts up to 20 (9 + 8, 18 − 9) and be able to give the answers very quickly. Many school districts expect the times tables to be memorized by the end of third grade, and certainly almost all school districts expect the tables to be memorized by the end of fourth grade.

If your child is still hesitating, counting on fingers, or searching the ceiling for the proper answer, it's past time to take action. She needs to know these facts almost as quickly as she knows her name.

First, take an inventory of all the addition and subtraction facts to make sure your child knows what they are. If your child is shaky or slow on a few, concentrate on getting her up to speed on these. Ask math facts while driving in the car. Have your child join you in the kitchen while you cook for a Math Facts Blitz.

When you're sure she thoroughly knows addition and subtraction through 20, forge ahead to the times tables. Have your child recite by twos, by threes, by fours. Once she knows these well, you can begin to mix up facts.

## What Tests May Ask

You can be sure standardized tests will ask questions based on a knowledge of the math facts, together with specifics on regrouping, short division, long division, and operating with fractions.

> **Tip**
>
> If your child needs extra help on basic math facts, visit a teaching supplies store and look for math facts set to music or set to rap. Setting material to music is an excellent way to cement facts in memory in a permanent way. Whatever method you use, strive for accuracy first, and then speed.

## Regrouping

Once you're sure your child knows the basics, she can concentrate on the processes needed in fifth-grade mathematics. The first multistep process to learn is regrouping in addition, subtraction, and multiplication problems. You probably called this carrying and borrowing; regrouping is the modern term for the same thing.

Since regrouping is usually introduced in second grade, your child probably knows all about the process, but her speed on the math facts will make the process much easier. If you notice that your child understands regrouping but makes errors because she doesn't align the numbers properly, buy her some graph paper and have her copy her problems with one number to a box. If your child writes slowly or sloppily, copy the problems out of the book yourself and have her do the actual problems. Remember: What's important now is the process; legibility is a problem for another day.

## Long and Short Division

Long and short division are important skills in the fifth grade curriculum. First your child needs to remember the steps in long division:

1. Divide
2. Multiply
3. Subtract
4. Bring Down

If your child has trouble remembering the steps, try using a mnemonic to help her remember the steps in order: **D**ad, **M**om, **S**ister, **B**rother. Write these words on an index card. If you like, choose a family in which Dad is older than Mom and with an older sister and younger brother; cut out pictures of their faces, and paste them on the index card. Linking the names "Dad, Mom…" with age (Dad is oldest, Mom comes next) will help keep the mnemonic terms in order. You can laminate the card if you wish. The card should look like this:

> **Dad**
> **Mom**
> **Sister**
> **Brother**

A simpler mnemonic may help. Make up a nonsense sentence using the important letters: Dogs May Slurp Beans. Have your fifth grader make up her own nonsense mnemonic—it may help her remember it!

With the card or mnemonic phrase as a memory aid and the math facts mastered, your child needs to practice until the process is well-learned.

## Fractions

Your fifth grader should be able to add and subtract fractions with like and unlike denominators. The biggest problem in this area is finding the lowest common denominator. Again, appeal to your child's imagination. You might ask her to be a detective to find out the true name of a number who has been using a false alias.

PARENT: Tonight you have to add fractions that have unlike denominators, like adding $\frac{1}{2}$ and $\frac{1}{4}$.

CHILD: Yeah, and I just don't get it.

PARENT: Well, the trouble is that these two numbers have to have the same denominator before you can add them, and even worse, one of the numbers is an imposter.

CHILD: What is an imposter?

PARENT: It's someone with a false identity, pretending to be someone they really aren't. Usually the imposter is the one with the lower denominator.

CHILD: So how do you figure out the true identity?

PARENT: Well, you have to find another name for one of the fractions that is its true identity. Let's look at the ½ in our problem about ½ and ¼. Maybe the ½ really has the same last name as the ¼, which is "fourth." Write ½ and next to it write /4. Now ½ is the same as how many fourths? (Use shaded squares if needed to show the concept.)

CHILD: Well, ½ is the same as ²⁄4.

PARENT: You did it! In this problem, the true name of ½ was ²⁄4. Now both of your fractions have the same last name, "fourth," and you can add them. Now let me show you a math shortcut to find out the true identities of fractions in a hurry.

Then proceed to show the child the method for converting any fraction into a new fraction with a different denominator:

1. Find the lowest common denominator by systematically guessing.

2. Divide the old denominator into the lowest common denominator.

3. Multiply that number by the old numerator.

4. Voila! You have the new numerator.

Once again, the child who isn't secure in her math facts won't be able to give all her energy to learning the process.

Warn your child that many standardized tests will ask her to actually compute the answers to each problem instead of guessing. They may have an "NG" option, which stands for "Answer Not Given." Some children are confused by this and don't know what to do if they compute an answer that isn't one of the options.

## Practice Skills: Math Computation

**Directions:** Read each problem and choose the correct answer.

**1**   $30 + 16 + 3 =$
- Ⓐ  46
- Ⓑ  49
- Ⓒ  59
- Ⓓ  NG

**2**   $4712 + 6298 =$
- Ⓐ  11,100
- Ⓑ  10,100
- Ⓒ  10,010
- Ⓓ  11,010
- Ⓔ  NG

**3**   $\$34.19 + \$62.01$
- Ⓐ  $96.20
- Ⓑ  $106.20
- Ⓒ  $97.20
- Ⓓ  $96.10
- Ⓔ  NG

**4**   $82.43 + 19.69 =$
- Ⓐ  201.12
- Ⓑ  101.12
- Ⓒ  100.12
- Ⓓ  102.12
- Ⓔ  NG

**5**   510
     25
     37
   + 42
- Ⓐ  714
- Ⓑ  514
- Ⓒ  513
- Ⓓ  715
- Ⓔ  NG

**6** $4.1 + 0.8 =$
- Ⓐ 4.9
- Ⓑ 4.18
- Ⓒ 5.9
- Ⓓ 5.18
- Ⓔ NG

**7** $17 + \underline{\phantom{00}} = 54$
- Ⓐ 71
- Ⓑ 47
- Ⓒ 37
- Ⓓ 31
- Ⓔ NG

**8** $2/9 + 7/9 =$
- Ⓐ $5/9$
- Ⓑ $9/9$
- Ⓒ $8/9$
- Ⓓ $9/7$
- Ⓔ NG

**9** $1\,4/7 + 3\,3/7 =$
- Ⓐ $4\,6/7$
- Ⓑ $2\,1/7$
- Ⓒ 6
- Ⓓ 5
- Ⓔ NG

**10** $1/6 + 1/12 =$
- Ⓐ $1/4$
- Ⓑ $3/12$
- Ⓒ $3/6$
- Ⓓ both A and B
- Ⓔ NG

**11** $\begin{array}{r} 5038 \\ -\ 665 \\ \hline \end{array}$
- Ⓐ 4373
- Ⓑ 5463
- Ⓒ 4473
- Ⓓ 5473
- Ⓔ NG

**12** $\begin{array}{r} \$63.25 \\ -\ 12.47 \\ \hline \end{array}$
- Ⓐ $60.78
- Ⓑ $61.78
- Ⓒ $51.78
- Ⓓ $51.68
- Ⓔ NG

**13** $42 - \underline{\phantom{00}} = 9$
- Ⓐ 51
- Ⓑ 33
- Ⓒ 23
- Ⓓ 32
- Ⓔ NG

**14** $\begin{array}{r} 7\,4/5 \\ -\ 2/5 \\ \hline \end{array}$
- Ⓐ $7\,1/5$
- Ⓑ $7\,2/5$
- Ⓒ $8\,1/5$
- Ⓓ $8\,2/5$
- Ⓔ NG

**15** $7/8 - 5/8 =$
- Ⓐ $3/8$
- Ⓑ $12/8$
- Ⓒ $1\,1/2$
- Ⓓ $2/8$
- Ⓔ NG

**16** $5/6 + 1/3 =$
- Ⓐ $1/2$
- Ⓑ $1\,1/6$
- Ⓒ $4/3$
- Ⓓ 1
- Ⓔ NG

**17** $3 \times 6 \times 2 =$
- Ⓐ 11
- Ⓑ 9
- Ⓒ 24
- Ⓓ 36
- Ⓔ NG

**18**  $403 \times 7$

    Ⓐ  2828
    Ⓑ  2821
    Ⓒ  410
    Ⓓ  2829
    Ⓔ  NG

**19**  285
    $\times 62$

    Ⓐ  17,570
    Ⓑ  2,280
    Ⓒ  18,670
    Ⓓ  17,670
    Ⓔ  NG

**20**  4.5
    $\times 0.7$

    Ⓐ  3.15
    Ⓑ  5.2
    Ⓒ  3.8
    Ⓓ  0.315
    Ⓔ  NG

**21**  $54 \div 3 =$

    Ⓐ  16
    Ⓑ  51
    Ⓒ  18
    Ⓓ  17
    Ⓔ  NG

**22**  $6 \overline{)370}$

    Ⓐ  60 R 4
    Ⓑ  61 R 4
    Ⓒ  61 R 3
    Ⓓ  61
    Ⓔ  NG

**23**  $58 \div 7 =$

    Ⓐ  8
    Ⓑ  8 R 3
    Ⓒ  8 R 1
    Ⓓ  9
    Ⓔ  NG

**24**  $32 \overline{)960}$

    Ⓐ  31
    Ⓑ  310 R 5
    Ⓒ  20
    Ⓓ  30
    Ⓔ  NG

(See page 102 for answer key.)

# CHAPTER 9

# Math Applications

I find the most "math shock" among parents when they realize what their fifth graders are being taught in the area of math applications. Many parents solemnly assure me that they've lived for 35 years without ever having heard of a line of symmetry.

When they realize that their children are expected to understand words like *congruence* or find volumes in cubic units, they insist that they didn't cover this material until tenth grade. Many other parents' eyes glaze over when metric measurement units are introduced. They haven't the faintest idea whether a breadbox would be measured in centimeters or in meters.

Of course, parental shock is understandable. Our children truly are learning material at earlier and earlier ages. Is this good or harmful? The final answers aren't in yet, but in the meantime, your child will be taking a standardized test soon and this material will be included. In this chapter, we talk about all of the basic math applications with which fifth graders should be familiar.

## Education Goals for Fifth Graders

Your fifth grader should have a working knowledge of basic math facts, geometry, measurement, and word problem solving. He should be able to tell time, understand money and make change easily, and handle both metric and non-metric units of measure.

## What You and Your Child Can Do

I often think of the mind as a computer. Your brain can handle two tasks at once, but you work more slowly than if you were doing one thing at a time. If your child knows the math facts and has to devote only a tiny bit of effort to come up with the answer to 6 times 8, all the rest of his working memory is left over to be applied to figuring out the problem. Once again, drill those math facts and be sure your child has a clear idea of what the math terms mean in the problems.

## What Tests May Ask

On most major standardized tests, there are three main areas tested in the section known as math applications: geometry, measurement, and problem solving.

The broken record begins to play: "Vocabulary. Vocabulary. Vocabulary. Math facts. Math facts. Math facts."

When a child is faced with test items in the area of math applications, he usually sees word problems composed of several sentences of math vocabulary. If your child doesn't know the definitions of *perimeter* or *area,* his answer will be wrong, even if he's perfectly capable of multiplying length by width. If he knows how the process of finding an area works, but doesn't know his math facts, his knowledge won't do him any good.

## Geometry

Many people say they were terrific in math—except for the year they had geometry. Other people insist they were the worst student in every math class with one exception: geometry. For some reason, geometry just doesn't seem to fit in with the rest of math.

Some research suggests that this is because learning geometry calls on different parts of the brain. Whatever the reason, you may find that your child reacts very differently to geometry problems than to any other type of math.

## What Your Fifth Grader Should Be Learning

The first obstacle to a good grasp of geometry is a weak math vocabulary. If you're going to do well in geometry, you have to know what polygons, trapezoids, and congruent triangles are. Fortunately, these shapes are all around us.

Luckily, most geometry questions can be answered if the child at this age knows what the terms mean. A few formulas should also be known. Your child should be able to find the perimeter and area of regular shapes like squares and rectangles. He should also be able to find the diameter and radius of a circle.

## What You Can Do

The first thing you can do is make sure your child knows the vocabulary covered in the geometry section of his math textbook. Common terms include: intersection, perimeter, area, diameter, radius, right angle, acute angle, obtuse angle, line of symmetry, line segment, ray, parallel, perpendicular, congruent, and similar.

Try using objects in your environment to review these terms. For example, hold up a CD and a coin and point out that these two shapes are similar, but only two CDs or two nickels could be considered congruent. While sitting in traffic behind a FedEx truck, point out similar

capital E's, squares, intersecting lines, a diamond with two lines of symmetry, and parallel lines.

Try finding shapes as you are driving down the highway. Don't just stick with the easy ones, like squares and circles. Go for rectangular prisms, pyramids, rays, and line segments. Look for lines that are parallel and perpendicular. Using this vocabulary will really strengthen a geometric sense. Don't be worried if you have never heard of a line of symmetry. Look it up in the dictionary or in your child's math book.

If your child needs work on finding area or perimeter, let him measure real objects and then compute the area or perimeter. Kids usually love to measure things, and it's much easier to remember something that you've done than something you've only read about in a book.

## Practice Skills: Geometry

**Directions:** Read each problem and choose the correct answer.

1   Compute the perimeter of the rectangle below in meters.

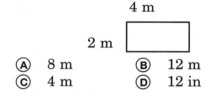

   Ⓐ  8 m     Ⓑ  12 m
   Ⓒ  4 m     Ⓓ  12 in

2   The area of the figure below is

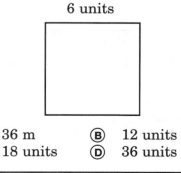

   Ⓐ  36 m     Ⓑ  12 units
   Ⓒ  18 units     Ⓓ  36 units

**3** How many pairs of lines shown below intersect?

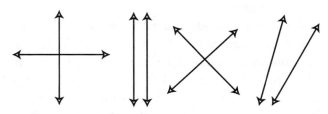

- Ⓐ one
- Ⓑ two
- Ⓒ three
- Ⓓ four

**4** Which of these shows a line of symmetry?

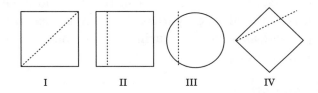

- Ⓐ I
- Ⓑ II
- Ⓒ III
- Ⓓ IV

**5** Which of these is an obtuse angle?

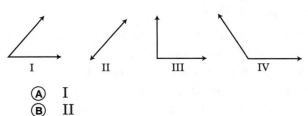

- Ⓐ I
- Ⓑ II
- Ⓒ III
- Ⓓ IV

**6** The pyramids in Egypt are shaped most like:

- Ⓐ a cube
- Ⓑ a sphere
- Ⓒ a triangular prism
- Ⓓ a rectangular prism

**7** Which of these lines are parallel?

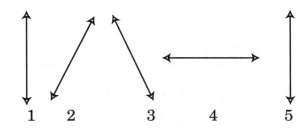

- Ⓐ 1 and 3
- Ⓑ 1 and 5
- Ⓒ 2 and 3
- Ⓓ 4 and 5

**8** Which pair of shapes is congruent?

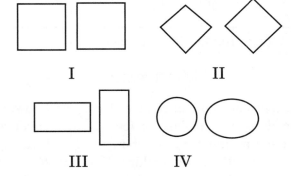

- Ⓐ I
- Ⓑ II
- Ⓒ III
- Ⓓ IV

**9** The circle below has a radius AB of 2 centimeters. How long is the diameter?

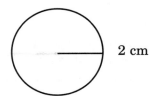

2 cm

Ⓐ  8 cm
Ⓑ  4 m
Ⓒ  2 m
Ⓓ  4 cm

**10** What is the volume of the shape below?

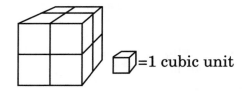

=1 cubic unit

Ⓐ  4 cubic units
Ⓑ  16 cubic units
Ⓒ  6 cubic units
Ⓓ  8 cubic units

(See page 102 for answer key.)

## Measurement

Measurement includes more than just knowing the details of inches or feet. It also involves understanding time, temperature, and money. Even in fifth grade, children are still learning the fine points of these different types of measurements.

## What Your Fifth Grader Should Be Learning

By fifth grade, children are expected to be able to measure using units of time, money, temperature, volume, length, and width. They should understand both metric units and inches, feet, miles, gallons, and so on; and they should be able to quickly combine coins and count out different amounts: one quarter, one nickel, and three pennies.

An important idea in fifth grade is whether units are "reasonable." For example, is it reasonable to measure cloth in miles? Is it reasonable to sell milk in liter containers? Many adults aren't comfortable with metric measurement, but think of your child's math book as your chance to expand your horizons. You never know when you might win a trip to Paris and you'll have to compute the kilometers from the airport to your hotel!

## What You Can Do

Measure distances and lengths using real objects, at home or in the car. Be sure you have a traditional ruler, yardstick, or tape measure, as well as some measuring device that shows metric units.

### Estimation

Ask your children to estimate: How high do you think that house is? How far do you estimate it is around this track? Let your child practice converting between measures: feet to yards, meters to centimeters. Children usually enjoy measurement because it's concrete and novel.

### In the Kitchen

Practice with volume measurements in the kitchen: gallons, cups, pints, and quarts. Send your child on a scavenger hunt for measuring words in the pantry, and he will soon notice metric units as well as quarts and pounds. "Jared, find some way I could pour out a pint of apple juice. Find me something that's measured in ounces."

## Temperature

When reviewing temperature, let your child use your digital thermometer to measure the temperatures of ice water, a cup of tea, or his own body temperature. Children love to conduct experiments like this, and your child will be getting practice reading a scale. Be sure to point out Fahrenheit and Celsius.

## Money Skills

Money skills are best taught in real, everyday situations. By now your child should be able to make change for amounts over $1, so be sure to let him practice in the store. Have him figure out how much change he should get, and then verify it at the cash register.

Many parents have their children count out ice cream money or money for the book order from a bowl of change. You could also practice making change: "If the Nutty Buddy costs $1.45 and I only have $2 to give you, how much change will you bring home?" Assure your savvy child that the correct answer is not "Nothing!"

## Elapsed Time

One measurement skill that's very hard for many children is the area of elapsed time. You probably remember the dreaded train that travels from New York to Baltimore. It was running when you were a child and it continues to run today. In an elapsed time problem, the child is told when the train leaves New York and how long the trip is expected to take. So what time will that exhausted man from Maryland get home?

Another type of elapsed time problem deals with a child who is waiting for lunch. You know what time it is now and what time his class will go to lunch. The question is how much longer he has to wait (and the answer is not "Forever"). There are many opportunities for you to practice elapsed time during the day in real situations:

It's 7:30. How long until your favorite show comes on TV?

Today is December fourth. How many more days until Christmas? How many more hours?

I want to sit down for supper at 6:30. Look at the kitchen clock and figure out how much longer until supper.

While we're discussing time, be sure that your child can tell time on analog as well as digital clocks. It's amazing how many children never become proficient with the old-fashioned timepieces because they can look at a digital watch and not have to work it out.

## Practice Skills: Measurement

**Directions:** Select the right equivalent from the possibilities given.

**11**  5 meters =
- (A) 50 centimeters
- (B) 500 centimeters
- (C) 5000 centimeters

**12**  Which one of these measures is the largest?
- (A) 3 gallons
- (B) 10 cups
- (C) 8 quarts
- (D) 30 cups

**13**  Which of these would best be measured in centimeters?
- (A) a football field
- (B) a football
- (C) a speck of dirt on the football field
- (D) 10 yards or a first down

**14**  Which of the following coin combinations does NOT equal $2?
- (A) 20 dimes
- (B) 40 nickels
- (C) 8 quarters
- (D) 10 nickels and 100 pennies

**15** Katie is flying from San Francisco to Atlanta to visit her aunt. The flight will take 4 hours and 15 minutes. The plane leaves at 11 a.m. When Katie lands in Atlanta, what time will it be in San Francisco?

(A) 3:45 p.m.
(B) 3:15 a.m.
(C) 3:15 p.m.
(D) 7:15 p.m.

**16** What temperature is shown on this thermometer?

(A) 64°
(B) 63°
(C) 62°
(D) 61°

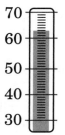

**17** About how long is this ribbon?

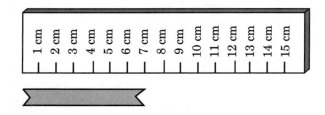

(A) 7 meters
(B) 7 inches
(C) 6 centimeters
(D) 7 centimeters

**18** Maggie went to see a showing of *Gone with the Wind*. The movie lasts 3 hours and 55 minutes. In addition, there is an intermission that lasts 30 minutes. If the movie starts at 4:15 p.m., what time should Maggie's mother come to pick her up?

(A) 7:10 p.m.
(B) 7:15 p.m.
(C) 8:15 p.m.
(D) 8:40 p.m.

**19** Matthew and John are practicing for a video game tournament. In the morning, they play for three hours. After lunch, they practice for two more hours until their father makes them go outside for some exercise. That evening, they compete for one more hour before bedtime. What fraction of the day was spent on video games?

(A) 1/4
(B) 1/8
(C) 1/6
(D) 1/3

**20** Which of these answers is closest to the length of the line above this ruler?

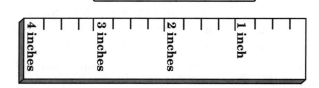

(A) 2³/4 inches
(B) 2 inches
(C) 2¹/4 inches
(D) 2¹/2 inches

(See page 102 for answer key.)

## Problem Solving

Problem solving is the Mount Everest of the arithmetic world. Your child has learned to climb the lower slopes by learning the math facts quickly and accurately. He has ascended through upper elevations by learning lots and lots of math vocabulary; and he's made it to the high ridges by learning multiple-step processes like long division, converting fractions and decimals, and figuring elapsed time. But if he is to reach the summit, he has to put all these pieces together in order to solve the problem. If any of the lower steps are weak, he'll never make it to the summit. There's just too much risk of a careless error along the way.

## What Your Fifth Grader Should Be Learning

Your fifth grader should be able to read a word problem of several sentences (often accompanied by a graph, table, or chart) and should be able to identify the bits of information provided in the problem. He should be able to state clearly what information the problem is asking him to give, and he should be able to differentiate necessary from extraneous facts given in the problem.

At this age, word problems may even include probability, such as predicting the probability of an event. For example, if a penny is tossed 20 times, about how many of those tosses will end up heads?

## What You Can Do

When your child makes a mistake on a word problem, have him do the problem aloud as you watch. It's usually fairly easy to identify the problem. If it's a matter of unknown vocabulary, a wrong math fact, or insufficient practice on a math process, you know what to do.

However, suppose your child simply freezes after reading a math word problem. The child simply doesn't know what to do with this word problem. You can teach your child a logical way to attack these tricky math challenges. Sometimes, providing a structure or a scaffold around the problem gives enough support for your child to solve it.

1.  Have your child read the problem aloud. If reading is a weak area, read the problem aloud yourself.

2.  Ask your child to identify all the facts that are given in the problem, in order.

3.  Ask your child to clearly state what answer is being asked for. Here's an example:

    Will is training for a 10K run. He began by running from his house to the lake, which is about 1.5 miles. Then he jogged around the lake. Will has been concerned that he runs much slower than his friends who run marathons. They usually run the five-mile lake distance in 30 minutes. Will took 50 minutes to finish the course. Then Will ran home. How far did Will run?

PARENT: List all the facts you got in this problem, but list them in order. Don't combine facts in one sentence. Just state each fact in its own sentence.

CHILD: Okay. Will is training for a 10K race. It is 1½ miles from his house to the lake. Will jogged once around the lake. Will runs more slowly than his serious running friends. His friends can run around the lake in 30 minutes. Will took 50 minutes to make it around the lake. He ended by running the 1½ miles home.

PARENT: That was great, but I think you missed one fact.

CHILD: Where? I think I got everything.

PARENT: Read the fifth sentence aloud and see if it tells you anything about the distance around the lake.

CHILD: Oh, here it is. It's 5 miles around the lake.

PARENT: Great! Now you have all your facts straight. Now tell me one more thing: What piece of information does the problem ask you to come up with?

CHILD: They want to know how far he ran.

PARENT: Do they just want to know how far he ran around the lake, or how far he ran in total?

CHILD: I'm not sure, but I think the problem would be too easy if they only wanted the distance around the lake. It must be the total miles.

PARENT: You're right. So what do you have to do to get a total?

CHILD: Well, you would have to add all the little pieces of the run, from home to the lake, around the lake, and then back home again. The answer must be, let's see … it's 8 miles!

The parent proceeded in a logical way to have the child lay out all the information and then identify the question being asked. However, there was one part of this problem solving that the parent didn't teach. The parent had to sit and wait while the light bulb snapped on in the child's mind. That's what was happening when the child was pausing and thinking after he said: "The answer must be…"

I'm not sure if you can directly teach this moment of awareness. I know that you can lead your child up to the moment, but it's very important to sit back quietly at this point and let your child think without being nudged or interrupted. If he doesn't make the connection, try to be patient. Drop back to a more concrete level if you can. Sketch a very quick map of Will's house and the lake and let your child label the distances. Then be silent for a moment and let your child think. Problem solving is a tough skill to master, so provide plenty of chances to practice.

Luckily, problem solving is a skill you can practice in the car or at the dinner table. Keep the numbers simple so that the calculations can be done mentally. But throw in extra unneeded facts and don't state each fact directly. Let your

child practice understanding what is implied. I found that making up word problems about family members and friends made this activity acceptable to my children. I also tried to choose humorous or outlandish situations. "Daniel hit his brother 9 times. Bill hit him back 17 times. How many more times did Bill hit than Daniel?" No, we shouldn't model violence, but you can make it clear that this is a joke. Besides, children love forbidden situations and humorous exaggeration.

## Practice Skills: Problem Solving

**Directions:** Read each problem and choose the correct answer.

21  There are 18 marbles in a jar. The marbles are either black or white. Fifty percent of the marbles are white. How many black marbles are in the jar?

   Ⓐ  8
   Ⓑ  9
   Ⓒ  10
   Ⓓ  Not Given

22  Ann's teacher keeps a jar of Jolly Ranchers on her desk. Ann has learned all her multiplication and division facts on a timed test, so she's allowed to close her eyes and reach into the jar to get a piece of candy. There are 10 pieces of candy in the jar: 2 are apple, which is Ann's favorite flavor. Three are watermelon, which she likes pretty well, but 5 are the flavor she hates: lemon! What are Ann's chances of choosing her favorite flavor?

   Ⓐ  3 out of 10
   Ⓑ  1 out of 2
   Ⓒ  5 out of 10
   Ⓓ  1 out of 5

**23** The graph below shows how many students at Peachtree Elementary School are collectors. If there are 800 students at the school, how many of them collect Beanie Babies?

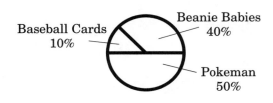

Baseball Cards 10%  Beanie Babies 40%  Pokeman 50%

- Ⓐ 400
- Ⓑ 80
- Ⓒ 320
- Ⓓ 240

**24** Using the graph in problem 23, how many of the students at Peachtree collect baseball cards?

- Ⓐ 80
- Ⓑ 400
- Ⓒ 240
- Ⓓ 8

**Directions:** Use the graph below to answer questions 25 through 28.

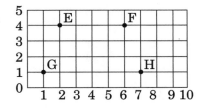

**25** What are the coordinates of point F?

- Ⓐ (5, 3)
- Ⓑ (4, 6)
- Ⓒ (7, 1)
- Ⓓ (6, 4)

**26** What point is at (2, 4)?

- Ⓐ G
- Ⓑ H
- Ⓒ E
- Ⓓ F

**27** Suppose you connected points E-F, G-H, E-G, and F-H. The figure that you formed is:

- Ⓐ a polygon
- Ⓑ a rectangle
- Ⓒ a trapezoid
- Ⓓ A and C

**28** If point G were moved two units to the right, what would its new coordinates be?

- Ⓐ (1, 3)
- Ⓑ (2, 3)
- Ⓒ (3, 1)
- Ⓓ (4, 1)

**Directions:** Study this graph to answer questions 29 and 30.

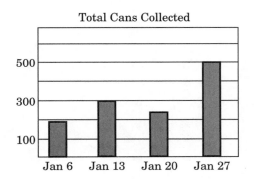

Total Cans Collected

**29** The children at Mason Elementary are collecting canned goods for a local food bank. The graph above shows how many cans were collected on the Fridays in January.

On which day was the number of cans collected closest to 200 cans?

- Ⓐ Jan. 6
- Ⓑ Jan. 13
- Ⓒ Jan. 20
- Ⓓ Jan. 27

**30** The total number of cans collected was about:

- Ⓐ 1000
- Ⓑ 1200
- Ⓒ 1250
- Ⓓ 1300

(See page 102 for answer key.)

# Web Sites and Resources for More Information

## Homework

### Homework Central
http://www.HomeworkCentral.com
Terrific site for students, parents, and teachers, filled with information, projects, and more.

### Win the Homework Wars
(Sylvan Learning Centers)
http://www.educate.com/online/qa_peters.html

## Reading and Grammar Help

### Born to Read: How to Raise a Reader
http://www.ala.org/alsc/raise_a_reader.html

### Guide to Grammar and Writing
http://webster.commnet.edu/hp/pages/darling/grammar.htm
Help with "plague words and phrases," grammar FAQs, sentence parts, punctuation, rules for common usage.

### Internet Public Library: Reading Zone
http://www.ipl.org/cgi-bin/youth/youth.out

### Keeping Kids Reading and Writing
http://www.tiac.net/users/maryl/

### U.S. Dept. of Education: Helping Your Child Learn to Read
http://www.ed.gov/pubs/parents/Reading/index.html

## Math Help

### Center for Advancement of Learning
http://www.muskingum.edu/%7Ecal/database/Math2.html
Substitution and memory strategies for math.

### Center for Advancement of Learning
http://www.muskingum.edu/%7Ecal/database/Math1.html
General tips and suggestions.

### Math.com
http://www.math.com
The world of math online.

### Math.com
http://www.math.com/student/testprep.html
Get ready for standardized tests.

### Math.com: Homework Help in Math
http://www.math.com/students/homework.html

### Math.com: Math for Homeschoolers
http://www.math.com/parents/homeschool.html

### The Math Forum: Problems and Puzzles
http://forum.swarthmore.edu/library/resource_types/problems_puzzles
Lots of fun math puzzles and problems for grades K through 12.

### The Math Forum: Math Tips and Tricks
http://forum.swarthmore.edu/k12/mathtips/mathtips.html

## Tips on Testing

### Books on Test Preparation
http://www.testbooksonline.com/preHS.asp
This site provides printed resources for parents who wish to help their children prepare for standardized school tests.

### Core Knowledge Web Site
http://www.coreknowledge.org/
Site dedicated to providing resources for parents; based on the books of E. D. Hirsch, Jr., who wrote the *What Your X Grader Needs to Know* series.

### Family Education Network
http://www.familyeducation.com/article/0,1120,
1-6219,00.html
This report presents some of the arguments against current standardized testing practices in the public schools. The site also provides links to family activities that help kids learn.

### Math.com
http://www.math.com/students/testprep.html
Get ready for standardized tests.

### Standardized Tests
http://arc.missouri.edu/k12/
K through 12 assessment tools and know-how.

## Parents: Testing in Schools

### KidSource: Talking to Your Child's Teacher about Standardized Tests
http://www.kidsource.com/kidsource/content2/
talking.assessment.k12.4.html
This site provides basic information to help parents understand their children's test results and provides pointers for how to discuss the results with their children's teachers.

### eSCORE.com: State Test and Education Standards
http://www.eSCORE.com
Find out if your child meets the necessary requirements for your local schools. A Web site with experts from Brazelton Institute and Harvard's Project Zero.

### Overview of States' Assessment Programs
http://ericae.net/faqs/

### Parent Soup
### Education Central: Standardized Tests
http://www.parentsoup.com/edcentral/testing
A parent's guide to standardized testing in the schools, written from a parent advocacy standpoint.

### National Center for Fair and Open Testing, Inc. (FairTest)
342 Broadway
Cambridge, MA 02139
(617) 864-4810
http://www.fairtest.org

### National Parent Information Network
http://npin.org

### Publications for Parents from the U.S. Department of Education
http://www.ed.gov/pubs/parents/
An ever-changing list of information for parents available from the U.S. Department of Education.

### State of the States Report
http://www.edweek.org/sreports/qc99/states/
indicators/in-intro.htm
A report on testing and achievement in the 50 states.

## Testing: General Information

### Academic Center for Excellence
http://www.acekids.com

### American Association for Higher Education Assessment
http://www.aahe.org/assessment/web.htm

### American Educational Research Association (AERA)
http://aera.net
An excellent link to reports on American education, including reports on the controversy over standardized testing.

### American Federation of Teachers
555 New Jersey Avenue, NW
Washington, D.C. 20011

## Association of Test Publishers Member Products and Services
http://www.testpublishers.org/memserv.htm

## Education Week on the Web
http://www.edweek.org

## ERIC Clearinghouse on Assessment and Evaluation
1131 Shriver Lab
University of Maryland
College Park, MD 20742
http://ericae.net
A clearinghouse of information on assessment and education reform.

## FairTest: The National Center for Fair and Open Testing
http://fairtest.org/facts/ntfact.htm
http://fairtest.org/
The National Center for Fair and Open Testing is an advocacy organization working to end the abuses, misuses, and flaws of standardized testing and to ensure that evaluation of students and workers is fair, open, and educationally sound. This site provides many links to fact sheets, opinion papers, and other sources of information about testing.

## National Congress of Parents and Teachers
700 North Rush Street
Chicago, Illinois 60611

## National Education Association
1201 16th Street, NW
Washington, DC 20036

## National School Boards Association
http://www.nsba.org
A good source for information on all aspects of public education, including standardized testing.

## Testing Our Children: A Report Card on State Assessment Systems
http://www.fairtest.org/states/survey.htm
Report of testing practices of the states, with graphical links to the states and a critique of fair testing practices in each state.

## Trends in Statewide Student Assessment Programs: A Graphical Summary
http://www.ccsso.org/survey96.html
Results of annual survey of states' departments of public instruction regarding their testing practices.

## U.S. Department of Education
http://www.ed.gov/

## Web Links for Parents Who Want to Help Their Children Achieve
http://www.liveandlearn.com/learn.html
This page offers many Web links to free and for-sale information and materials for parents who want to help their children do well in school. Titles include such free offerings as the Online Colors Game and questionnaires to determine whether your child is ready for school.

## What Should Parents Know about Standardized Testing in the Schools?
http://www.rusd.k12.ca.us/parents/standard.html
An online brochure about standardized testing in the schools, with advice regarding how to become an effective advocate for your child.

### Test Publishers Online

## ACT: Information for Life's Transitions
http://www.act.org

## American Guidance Service, Inc.
http://www.agsnet.com

## Ballard & Tighe Publishers
http://www.ballard-tighe.com

## Consulting Psychologists Press
http://www.cpp-db.com

## CTB McGraw-Hill
http://www.ctb.com

## Educational Records Bureau
http://www.erbtest.org/index.html

## Educational Testing Service
http://www.ets.org

**General Educational Development (GED) Testing Service**
http://www.acenet.edu/calec/ged/home.html

**Harcourt Brace Educational Measurement**
http://www.hbem.com

**Piney Mountain Press—A Cyber-Center for Career and Applied Learning**
http://www.pineymountain.com

**ProEd Publishing**
http://www.proedinc.com

**Riverside Publishing Company**
http://www.hmco.com/hmco/riverside

**Stoelting Co.**
http://www.stoeltingco.com

**Sylvan Learning Systems, Inc.**
http://www.educate.com

**Touchstone Applied Science Associates, Inc. (TASA)**
http://www.tasa.com

## Tests Online

(*Note:* We don't endorse tests; some may not have technical documentation. Evaluate the quality of any testing program before making decisions based on its use.)

**Edutest, Inc.**
http://www.edutest.com
Edutest is an Internet-accessible testing service that offers criterion-referenced tests for elementary school students, based upon the standards for K through 12 learning and achievement in the states of Virginia, California, and Florida.

**Virtual Knowledge**
http://www.smarterkids.com
This commercial service, which enjoys a formal partnership with Sylvan Learning Centers, offers a line of skills assessments for preschool through grade 9 for use in the classroom or the home. For free online sample tests, see the Virtual Test Center.

# Read More about It

Abbamont, Gary W. *Test Smart: Ready-to-Use Test-Taking Strategies and Activities for Grades 5–12. Upper Saddle River,* NJ: Prentice Hall Direct, 1997.

Cookson, Peter W., and Joshua Halberstam. *A Parent's Guide to Standardized Tests in School: How to Improve Your Child's Chances for Success.* New York: Learning Express, 1998.

Frank, Steven, and Stephen Frank. *Test-Taking Secrets: Study Better, Test Smarter, and Get Great Grades (The Backpack Study Series).* Holbrook, MA: Adams Media Corporation, 1998.

Gilbert, Sara Dulaney. *How to Do Your Best on Tests: A Survival Guide.* New York: Beech Tree Books, 1998.

Gruber, Gary. *Dr. Gary Gruber's Essential Guide to Test-Taking for Kids, Grades 3–5.* New York: William Morrow & Co., 1986.

———. *Gary Gruber's Essential Guide to Test-Taking for Kids, Grades 6, 7, 8, 9.* New York: William Morrow & Co., 1997.

Leonhardt, Mary. *99 Ways to Get Kids to Love Reading and 100 Books They'll Love.* New York: Crown, 1997.

———. *Parents Who Love Reading, Kids Who Don't: How It Happens and What You Can Do about It.* New York: Crown, 1995.

McGrath, Barbara B. *The Baseball Counting Book.* Watertown, MA: Charlesbridge, 1999.

———. *More M&M's Brand Chocolate Candies Math.* Watertown, MA: Charlesbridge, 1998.

Mokros, Janice R. *Beyond Facts & Flashcards: Exploring Math with Your Kids.* Portsmouth, NH: Heinemann, 1996.

Romain, Trevor, and Elizabeth Verdick. *True or False?: Tests Stink!* Minneapolis: Free Spirit Publishing Co., 1999.

Schartz, Eugene M. *How to Double Your Child's Grades in School: Build Brilliance and Leadership into Your Child—from Kindergarten to College—in Just 5 Minutes a Day.* New York: Barnes & Noble, 1999.

Taylor, Kathe, and Sherry Walton. *Children at the Center: A Workshop Approach to Standardized Test Preparation, K–8.* Portsmouth, NH: Heinemann, 1998.

Tobia, Sheila. *Overcoming Math Anxiety.* New York: W. W. Norton & Company, Inc., 1995.

Tufariello, Ann Hunt. *Up Your Grades: Proven Strategies for Academic Success.* Lincolnwood, IL: VGM Career Horizons, 1996.

Vorderman, Carol. *How Math Works.* Pleasantville, NY: Reader's Digest Association, Inc., 1996.

Zahler, Kathy A. *50 Simple Things You Can Do to Raise a Child Who Loves to Read.* New York: IDG Books, 1997.

# What Your Child's Test Scores Mean

Several weeks or months after your child has taken standardized tests, you will receive a report such as the TerraNova Home Report found in Figures 1 and 2. You will receive similar reports if your child has taken other tests. We briefly examine what information the reports include.

Look at the first page of the Home Report. Note that the chart provides labeled bars showing the child's performance. Each bar is labeled with the child's National Percentile for that skill area. When you know how to interpret them, national percentiles can be the most useful scores you encounter on reports such as this. Even when you are confronted with different tests that use different scale scores, you can always interpret percentiles the same way, regardless of the test. A percentile tells the percent of students who score at or below that level. A percentile of 25, for example, means that 25 percent of children taking the test scored at or below that score. (It also means that 75 percent of students scored above that score.) Note that the average is always at the 50th percentile.

On the right side of the graph on the first page of the report, the publisher has designated the ranges of scores that constitute average, above average, and below average. You can also use this slightly more precise key for interpreting percentiles:

| PERCENTILE RANGE | LEVEL |
|---|---|
| 2 and Below | Deficient |
| 3–8 | Borderline |
| 9–23 | Low Average |
| 24–75 | Average |
| 76–97 | High Average |
| 98 and Up | Superior |

The second page of the Home report provides a listing of the child's strengths and weaknesses, along with keys for mastery, partial mastery, and non-mastery of the skills. Scoring services determine these breakdowns based on the child's scores as compared with those from the national norm group.

Your child's teacher or guidance counselor will probably also receive a profile report similar to the TerraNova Individual Profile Report, shown in Figures 3 and 4. That report will be kept in your child's permanent record. The first aspect of this report to notice is that the scores are expressed both numerically and graphically.

First look at the score bands under National Percentile. Note that the scores are expressed as bands, with the actual score represented by a dot within each band. The reason we express the scores as bands is to provide an idea of the amount by which typical scores may vary for each student. That is, each band represents a

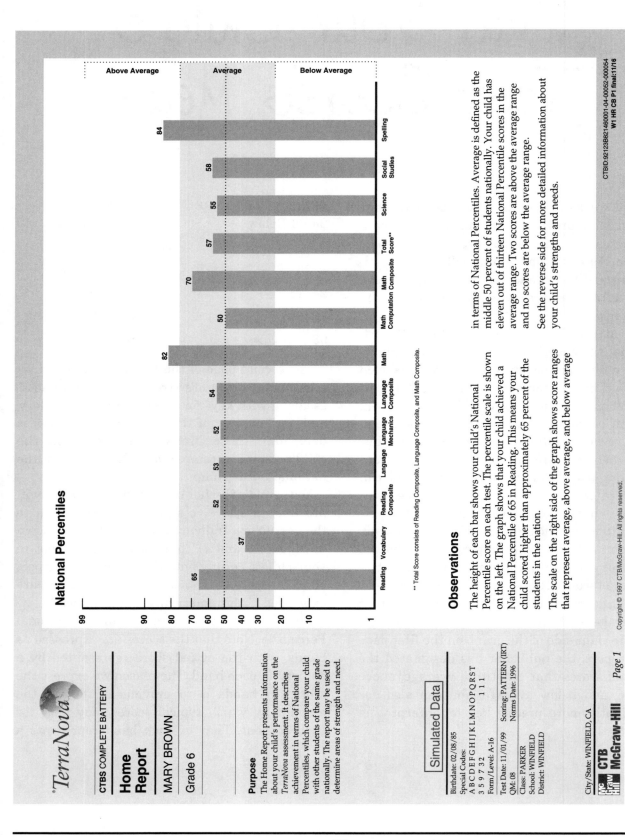

**Figure 1** (SOURCE: CTB/McGraw-Hill, copyright © 1997. All rights reserved. Reproduced with permission.)

*TerraNova*

**CTBS** COMPLETE BATTERY

**Home Report**

MARY BROWN

Grade 6

**Purpose**

This page of the Home Report presents information about your child's strengths and needs. This information is provided to help you monitor your child's academic growth.

Simulated Data

Birthdate: 02/08/85
Special Codes:
A B C D E F G H I J K L M N O P Q R S T
3 5 9 7 3 2                     1 1 1
Form/Level: A-16
Test Date: 11/01/99    Scoring: PATTERN (IRT)
QM: 08                 Norms Date: 1996

Class: PARKER
School: WINFIELD
District: WINFIELD

City/State: WINFIELD, CA

**CTB McGraw-Hill**

*Page 2*

**Strengths**

**Reading**
- Basic Understanding
- Analyze Text

**Vocabulary**
- Word Meaning
- Words in Context

**Language**
- Editing Skills
- Sentence Structure

**Language Mechanics**
- Sentences, Phrases, Clauses

**Mathematics**
- Computation and Numerical Estimation
- Operation Concepts

**Mathematics Computation**
- Add Whole Numbers
- Multiply Whole Numbers

**Science**
- Life Science
- Inquiry Skills

**Social Studies**
- Geographic Perspectives
- Economic Perspectives

**Spelling**
- Vowels
- Consonants

Key ● **Mastery**

**Needs**

**Reading**
- ◓ Evaluate and Extend Meaning
- ○ Identify Reading Strategies

**Vocabulary**
- ○ Multimeaning Words

**Language**
- ◓ Writing Strategies

**Language Mechanics**
- ○ Writing Conventions

**Mathematics**
- ◓ Measurement
- ◓ Geometry and Spatial Sense

**Mathematics Computation**
- ○ Percents

**Science**
- ○ Earth and Space Science

**Social Studies**
- ◓ Historical and Cultural Perspectives

**Spelling**
No area of needs were identified for this content area

Key ◓ **Partial Mastery**    ○ **Non-Mastery**

**General Interpretation**

The left column shows your child's best areas of performance. In each case, your child has reached mastery level. The column at the right shows the areas within each test section where your child's scores are the lowest. In these cases, your child has not reached mastery level, although he or she may have reached partial mastery.

CTBID:9212 3B82 1460001-04-00052-000054
W1 CB HR P2 Final:11/05

**Figure 2** (SOURCE: CTB/McGraw-Hill, copyright © 1997. All rights reserved. Reproduced with permission.)

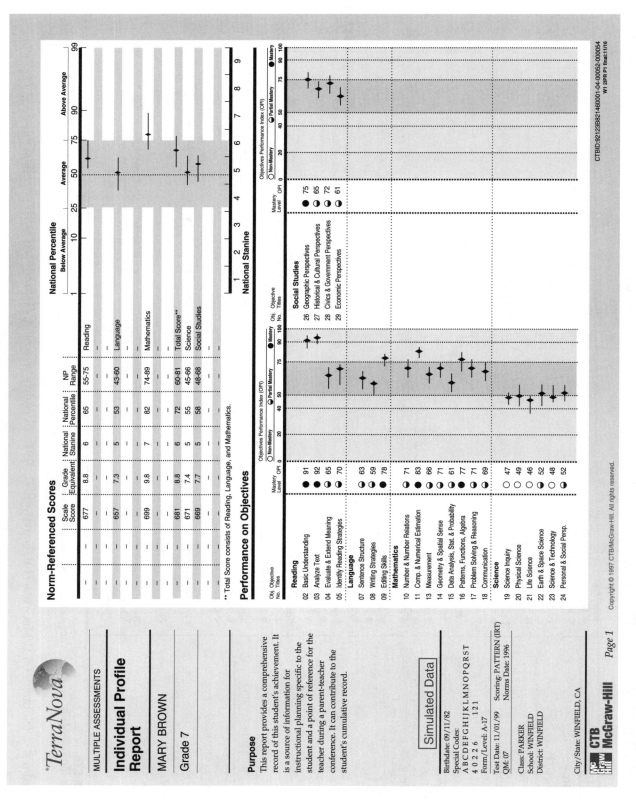

**Figure 3** (SOURCE: CTB/McGraw-Hill, copyright © 1997. All rights reserved. Reproduced with permission.)

# Observations

## Norm-Referenced Scores

The top section of the report presents information about this student's achievement in several different ways. The National Percentile (NP) data and graph indicate how this student performed compared to students of the same grade nationally. The National Percentile range indicates that if this student had taken the test numerous times the scores would have fallen within the range shown. The shaded area on the graph represents the average range of scores, usually defined as the middle 50 percent of students nationally. Scores in the area to the right of the shading are above the average range. Scores in the area to the left of the shading are below the average range.

In Reading, for example, this student achieved a National Percentile rank of 65. This student scored higher than 65 percent of the students nationally. This score is in the average range. This student has a total of five scores in the average range. One score is in the above average range. No scores are in the below average range.

## Performance on Objectives

The next section of the report presents performance on the objectives. Each objective is measured by a minimum of 4 items. The Objectives Performance Index (OPI) provides an estimate of the number of items that a student could be expected to answer correctly if there had been 100 items for that objective. The OPI is used to indicate mastery of each objective. An OPI of 75 and above characterizes Mastery. An OPI between 50 and 74 indicates Partial Mastery, and an OPI below 50 indicates Non-Mastery. The two-digit number preceding the objective title identifies the objective, which is fully described in the Teacher's Guide to *TerraNova*. The bands on either side of the diamonds indicate the range within which the student's test scores would fall if the student were tested numerous times.

In Reading, for example, this student could be expected to respond correctly to 91 out of 100 items measuring Basic Understanding. If this student had taken the test numerous times the OPI for this objective would have fallen between 82 and 93.

# Teacher Notes

---

MULTIPLE ASSESSMENTS

## Individual Profile Report

MARY BROWN

Grade 7

**Purpose**

The Observations section of the Individual Profile Report gives teachers and parents information to interpret this report. This page is a narrative description of the data on the other side.

*TerraNova*

Simulated Data

Birthdate: 09/11/82
Special Codes:
A B C D E F G H I J K L M N O P Q R S T
4 0 2 2 6      1 2 1
Form/Level: A-17

Test Date: 11/01/99      Scoring: PATTERN (IRT)
QM: 08                    Norms Date: 1996

Class: PARKER
School: WINFIELD
District: WINFIELD

City/State: WINFIELD, CA

**CTB McGraw-Hill**      *Page 2*      Copyright © 1997 CTB/McGraw-Hill. All rights reserved.

CTBID:921239B21460001-04-00052-000054
W1 IPR P2 final:11/05

**Figure 4** (SOURCE: CTB/McGraw-Hill, copyright © 1997. All rights reserved. Reproduced with permission.)

TerraNova™

MULTIPLE ASSESSMENTS

## Student Performance Level Report

KEN ALLEN

Grade 4

### Purpose

This report describes this student's achievement in terms of five performance levels for each content area. The meaning of these levels is described on the back of this page. Performance levels are a new way of describing achievement.

| Simulated Data |

Birthdate: 02/08/86
Special Codes:
A B C D E F G H I J K L M N O P Q R S T
3 5 9 7 3 2          1 1 1
Form/Level: A-14
Test Date: 04/15/97   Scoring: PATTERN (IRT)
QM: 31                 Norms Date: 1996

Class: SCHWARZ
School: WINFIELD
District: GREEN VALLEY

City/State: WINFIELD, CA

**CTB**
**McGraw-Hill**   *Page 1*

| Performance Levels | Reading | Language | Mathematics | Science | Social Studies |
|---|---|---|---|---|---|
| **5** Advanced | | | | | |
| **4** Proficient | | | | | |
| **3** Nearing Proficiency | ✓ | | | | ✓ |
| **2** Progressing | ✓ | ✓ | | ✓ | ✓ |
| **1** Step 1 | ✓ | ✓ | ✓ | ✓ | ✓ |

Partially Proficient

### Observations

Performance level scores provide a measure of what students *can do* in terms of the content and skills assessed by *TerraNova*, and typically found in curricula for Grades 3, 4, and 5. It is desirable to work towards achieving a Level 4 (Proficient) or Level 5 (Advanced) by the end of Grade 5.

The number of check marks indicates the performance level this student reached in each content area. For example, this student reached Level 3 in Reading and Social Studies.

The performance level indicates this student can perform the majority of what is described for that level and even more of what is described for the levels below. The student may also be capable of performing some of the things described in the next higher level, but not enough to have reached that level of performance.

For example, this student can perform the majority of what is described for Level 3 in Reading and even more of what is described for Level 2 and Level 1 in Reading. This student may also be capable of performing some of what is described for Level 4 in Reading.

For each content area look at the skills and knowledge described in the next higher level. These are the competencies this student needs to demonstrate to show academic growth.

**Figure 5**   (SOURCE: CTB/McGraw-Hill, copyright © 1997. All rights reserved. Reproduced with permission.)

| Performance Levels (Grades 3, 4, 5) | Reading | Language | Mathematics | Science | Social Studies |
|---|---|---|---|---|---|
| **5** Advanced | Students use analogies to generalize. They identify a paraphrase of concepts or ideas in texts. They can indicate thought processes that led them to a previous/alternate answer. In written responses, they demonstrate understanding of an implied theme, assess intent of passage information, and provide justification as well as support for their answers. | Students understand logical development in paragraph structure. They identify essential information from notes. They recognize the effect of prepositional phrases on subject-verb agreement. They find and correct at least 4 out of 6 errors when editing simple narratives. They correct run-on and incomplete sentences in more complex texts. They can eliminate all errors when editing their own work. | Students locate decimals on a number line; compute with decimals and fractions; read scale drawings; find areas; identify geometric transformations; construct and label bar graphs; find simple probabilities; find averages; use patterns in data to solve problems; use multiple strategies and concepts to solve unfamiliar problems; express mathematical ideas and explain the problem-solving process. | Students understand a broad range of grade level scientific concepts, such as the structure of Earth and instinctive behavior. They know terminology, such as decomposers, fossil fuel, eclipse, and buoyancy. Knowledge of more complex environmental issues includes, for example, the positive consequences of a forest fire. Students can process and interpret more detailed tables and graphs. They can suggest improvements to experimental design, such as running more trials. | Students consistently demonstrate skills such as synthesizing information from two sources (e.g., a document and a map). They show understanding of the democratic process and global environmental issues, and know the location of continents and major countries. They analyze and summarize information from multiple sources in early American history. They thoroughly explain both sides of an issue and give complete and detailed written answers to questions. |
| **4** Proficient | Students interpret figures of speech. They recognize paraphrase of text information and retrieve information to complete forms. In more complex texts, they identify themes, main ideas, or author purpose/point of view. They analyze and apply information in graphic and text form, make reasonable generalizations, and draw conclusions. In written responses, they can identify key elements from text. | Students select the best supporting sentences for a topic sentence. They use compound predicates to combine sentences. They identify simple subjects and predicates, recognize correct usage when confronted with two types of errors, and find and correct at least 3 out of 6 errors when editing simple narratives. They can edit their own work with only minor errors. | Students compare, order, and round whole numbers; know place value to thousands; identify fractions; use computation and estimation strategies; relate multiplication to addition; measure to nearest half-inch and centimeter; measure and find perimeters; estimate measures; find elapsed times; combine and subdivide shapes; identify parallel lines; interpret tables and graphs; solve two-step problems. | Students have a range of specific science knowledge, including details about animal adaptations and classification, states of matter, and the geology of Earth. They recognize scientific words such as habitat, gravity, and mass. They understand the usefulness of computers. They understand reasons for conserving natural resources. Understanding of experimentation includes analyzing purpose, interpreting data, and selecting tools to gather data. | Students demonstrate skills such as making inferences, using historical documents, and analyzing maps to determine the economic strengths of a region. They understand the function of currency in various cultures and supply and demand. They summarize information from multiple sources, recognize relationships, determine relevance of information, and show global awareness. They propose solutions to real-world problems and support ideas with appropriate details. |
| **3** Nearing Proficiency | Students use context clues and structural analysis to determine word meaning. They recognize homonyms and antonyms in grade-level text. They identify important details, sequence, cause and effect, and lessons embedded in the text. They interpret characters' feelings and apply information to new situations. In written responses, they can express an opinion and support it. | Students identify irrelevant sentences in paragraphs and select the best place to insert new information. They recognize faulty sentence construction. They can combine simple sentences with conjunctions and use simple subordination of phrases/clauses. They identify reference sources. They recognize correct conventions for dates, closings, and place names in informal correspondence. | Students identify even and odd numbers; subtract whole numbers with regrouping; multiply and divide by one-digit numbers; identify simple fractions; measure with ruler to nearest inch; tell time to nearest fifteen minutes; recognize and classify common shapes; recognize symmetry; subdivide shapes; complete bar graphs; extend numerical and geometric patterns; apply simple logical reasoning. | Students are familiar with the life cycles of plants and animals. They can identify an example of a cold-blooded animal. They infer what once existed from fossil evidence. They understand the water cycle. They know science and society issues such as recycling and sources of pollution. They can sequence technological advances. They extrapolate data, devise a simple classification scheme, and determine the purpose of a simple experiment. | Students demonstrate skills in organizing information. They use time lines, product and global maps, and cardinal directions. They understand simple cause and effect relationships and historical documents. They recognize events, associate holidays with events, and classify natural resources. They compare life in different times and understand some economic concepts related to products, jobs, and the environment. They give some detail in written responses. |
| **2** Progressing | Students identify synonyms for grade-level words, and use context clues to define common words. They make simple inferences and predictions based on text. They identify characters' feelings. They can transfer information from text to graphic form, or from graphic form to text. In written responses, they can provide limited support for their answers. | Students identify the use of correct verb tenses and supply verbs to complete sentences. They complete paragraphs by selecting an appropriate topic sentence. They select correct adjective forms. | Students know ordinal numbers; solve coin combination problems; count by tens; add whole numbers with regrouping; have basic estimation skills; understand addition property of zero; write and identify number sentences describing simple situations; read calendars; identify appropriate measurement tools; recognize congruent figures; use simple coordinate grids; read common tables and graphs. | Students recognize that plants decompose and become part of soil. They can classify a plant as a vegetable. They recognize that camouflage relates to survival. They recognize science terms such as hibernate. They have an understanding of human impact on the environment and are familiar with causes of pollution. They find the correct bar graph to represent given data and transfer data appropriate for middle elementary grades to a bar graph. | Students demonstrate simple information-processing skills such as using basic maps and keys. They recognize simple geographical terms, types of jobs, modes of transportation, and natural resources. They connect a human need with an appropriate community service. They identify some early famous presidents and know the capital of the United States. Their written answers are partially complete. |
| **1** Step 1 | Students select pictured representations of ideas and identify stated details contained in simple texts. In written responses, they can select and transfer information from charts. | Students supply subjects to complete sentences. They identify the correct use of pronouns. They edit for the correct use of end marks and initial capital letters, and identify the correct convention for greetings in letters. | Students read and recognize numbers to 1000; identify real-world use of numbers; add and subtract two-digit numbers without regrouping; identify addition situations; recognize and complete simple geometric and numerical patterns. | Students recognize basic adaptations for living in the water, identify an animal that is hatched from an egg, and associate an organism with its correct environment. They identify an object as metal. They have some understanding of conditions on the moon. They supply one way a computer can be useful. They associate an instrument like a telescope with a field of study. | Students are developing fundamental social studies skills such as locating and classifying basic information. They locate information in pictures and read and complete simple bar graphs related to social studies concepts and contexts. They can connect some city buildings with their functions and recognize certain historical objects. |

*Partially Proficient* (bracket spanning levels 1–3)

W1 SPLR P2:11/02

IMPORTANT: Each performance level, depicted on the other side, indicates the student can perform the majority of what is described for that level and even more of what is described for the levels below. The student may also be capable of performing some of the things described in the next higher level, but not enough to have reached that level.

**Figure 6** (SOURCE: CTB/McGraw-Hill, copyright © 1997. All rights reserved. Reproduced with permission.)

*confidence interval.* In these reports, we usually report either a 90 percent or 95 percent confidence interval. Interpret a confidence interval this way: Suppose we report a 90 percent confidence interval of 25 to 37. This means we estimate that, if the child took the test multiple times, we would expect that child's score to be in the 25 to 37 range 90 percent of the time.

Now look under the section titled Norm-Referenced Scores on the first page of the Individual Profile Report (Figure 3). The farthest column on the right provides the NP Range, which is the National Percentile scores represented by the score bands in the chart.

Next notice the column labeled Grade Equivalent. Theoretically, grade level equivalents equate a student's score in a skill area with the average grade placement of children who made the same score. Many psychologists and test developers would prefer that we stopped reporting grade equivalents, because they can be grossly misleading. For example, the average reading grade level of high school seniors as reported by one of the more popular tests is the eighth grade level. Does that mean that the nation's high school seniors cannot read? No. The way the test publisher calculated grade equivalents was to determine the average test scores for students in grades 4 to 6 and then simply extend the resulting prediction formula to grades 7 to 12. The result is that parents of average high school seniors who take the test in question would mistakenly believe that their seniors are reading four grade levels behind! Stick to the percentile in interpreting your child's scores.

Now look at the columns labeled Scale Score and National Stanine. These are two of a group of scores we also call *standard scores*. In reports for other tests, you may see other standard scores reported, such as Normal Curve Equivalents (NCEs), Z-Scores, and T-Scores. The IQ that we report on intelligence tests, for example, is a standard score. Standard scores are simply a way of expressing a student's scores in terms of the statistical properties of the scores from the norm group against which we are comparing the child. Although most psychologists prefer to speak in terms of standard scores among themselves, parents are advised to stick to percentiles in interpreting your child's performance.

Now look at the section of the report labeled Performance on Objectives. In this section, the test publisher reports how your child did on the various skills that make up each skills area. Note that the scores on each objective are expressed as a percentile band, and you are again told whether your child's score constitutes mastery, non-mastery, or partial mastery. Note that these scores are made up of tallies of sometimes small numbers of test items taken from sections such as Reading or Math. Because they are calculated from a much smaller number of scores than the main scales are (for example, Sentence Comprehension is made up of fewer items than overall Reading), their scores are less reliable than those of the main scales.

Now look at the second page of the Individual Profile Report (Figure 4). Here the test publisher provides a narrative summary of how the child did on the test. These summaries are computer-generated according to rules provided by the publisher. Note that the results descriptions are more general than those on the previous three report pages. But they allow the teacher to form a general picture of which students are performing at what general skill levels.

Finally, your child's guidance counselor may receive a summary report such as the TerraNova Student Performance Level Report. (See Figures 5 and 6.) In this report, the publisher explains to school personnel what skills the test assessed and generally how proficiently the child tested under each skill.

# Which States Require Which Tests

Tables 1 through 3 summarize standardized testing practices in the 50 states and the District of Columbia. This information is constantly changing; the information presented here was accurate as of the date of printing of this book. Many states have changed their testing practices in response to revised accountability legislation, while others have changed the tests they use.

**Table 1**   State Web Sites: Education and Testing

| STATE | GENERAL WEB SITE | STATE TESTING WEB SITE |
| --- | --- | --- |
| Alabama | http://www.alsde.edu/ | http://www.fairtest.org/states/al.htm |
| Alaska | www.educ.state.ak.us/ | http://www.eed.state.ak.us/tls/Performance Standards/ |
| Arizona | http://www.ade.state.az.us/ | http://www.ade.state.az.us/standards/ |
| Arkansas | http://arkedu.k12.ar.us/ | http://www.fairtest.org/states/ar.htm |
| California | http://goldmine.cde.ca.gov/ | http://ww.cde.ca.gov/cilbranch/sca/ |
| Colorado | http://www.cde.state.co.us/index_home.htm | http://www.cde.state.co.us/index_assess.htm |
| Connecticut | http://www.state.ct.us/sde | http://www.state.ct.us/sde/cmt/index.htm |
| Delaware | http://www.doe.state.de.us/ | http://www.doe.state.de.us/aab/index.htm |
| District of Columbia | http://www.k12.dc.us/dcps/home.html | http://www.k12.dc.us/dcps/data/data_frame2.html |
| Florida | http://www.firn.edu/doe/ | http://www.firn.edu/doe/sas/sasshome.htm |
| Georgia | http://www.doe.k12.ga.us/ | http://www.doe.k12.ga.us/sla/ret/recotest.html |
| Hawaii | http://kalama.doe.hawaii.edu/upena/ | http://www.fairtest.org/states/hi.htm |
| Idaho | http://www.sde.state.id.us/Dept/ | http://www.sde.state.id.us/instruct/ schoolaccount/statetesting.htm |
| Illinois | http://www.isbe.state.il.us/ | http://www.isbe.state.il.us/isat/ |
| Indiana | http://doe.state.in.us/ | http://doe.state.in.us/assessment/welcome.html |
| Iowa | http://www.state.ia.us/educate/index.html | (Tests Chosen Locally) |
| Kansas | http://www.ksbe.state.ks.us/ | http://www.ksbe.state.ks.us/assessment/ |
| Kentucky | http://www.kde.state.ky.us/ | http://www.kde.state.ky.us/oaa/ |
| Louisiana | http://www.doe.state.la.us/DOE/asps/home.asp | http://www.doe.state.la.us/DOE/asps/home.asp?I=HISTAKES |
| Maine | http://janus.state.me.us/education/homepage.htm | http://janus.state.me.us/education/mea/ meacompass.htm |
| Maryland | http://www.msde.state.md.us/ | http://www.fairtest.org/states/md.htm |
| Massachusetts | http://www.doe.mass.edu/ | http://www.doe.mass.edu/mcas/ |
| Michigan | http://www.mde.state.mi.us/ | http://www.mde.state.mi.us/off/meap/ |

| STATE | GENERAL WEB SITE | STATE TESTING WEB SITE |
|---|---|---|
| Minnesota | http://www.educ.state.mn.us/ | http://fairtest.org/states/mn.htm |
| Mississippi | http://mdek12.state.ms.us/ | http://fairtest.org/states/ms.htm |
| Missouri | http://services.dese.state.mo.us/ | http://fairtest.org/states/mo.htm |
| Montana | http://www.metnet.mt.gov/ | http://fairtest.org/states/mt.htm |
| Nebraska | http://nde4.nde.state.ne.us/ | http://www.edneb.org/IPS/AppAccrd/ApprAccrd.html |
| Nevada | http://www.nsn.k12.nv.us/nvdoe/ | http://www.nsn.k12.nv.us/nvdoe/reports/TerraNova.doc |
| New Hampshire | http://www.state.nh.us/doe/ | http://www.state.nh.us/doe/Assessment/assessme(NHEIAP).htm |
| New Jersey | http://ww.state.nj.us/education/ | http://www.state.nj.us/njded/stass/index.html |
| New Mexico | http://sde.state.nm.us/ | http://sde.state.nm.us/press/august30a.html |
| New York | http://www.nysed.gov/ | http://www.emsc.nysed.gov/ciai/assess.html |
| North Carolina | http://www.dpi.state.nc.us/ | http://www.dpi.state.nc.us/accountability/reporting/index.html |
| North Dakota | http://www.dpi.state.nd.us/dpi/index.htm | http://www.dpi.state.nd.us/dpi/reports/assess/assess.htm |
| Ohio | http://www.ode.state.oh.us/ | http://www.ode.state.oh.us/ca/ |
| Oklahoma | http://sde.state.ok.us/ | http://sde.state.ok.us/acrob/testpack.pdf |
| Oregon | http://www.ode.state.or.us// | http://www.ode.state.or.us/assmt/index.htm |
| Pennsylvania | http://www.pde.psu.edu/ http://instruct.ride.ri.net/ride_home_page.html | http://www.fairtest.org/states/pa.htm |
| Rhode Island | | |
| South Carolina | http://www.state.sc.us/sde/ | http://www.state.sc.us/sde/reports/terranov.htm |
| South Dakota | http://www.state.sd.us/state/executive/deca/ | http://www.state.sd.us/state/executive/deca/TA/McRelReport/McRelReports.htm |
| Tennessee | http://www.state.tn.us/education/ | http://www.state.tn.us/education/tsintro.htm |
| Texas | http://www.tea.state.tx.us/ | http://www.tea.state.tx.us/student.assessment/ |
| Utah | http://www.usoe.k12.ut.us/ | http://www.usoe.k12.ut.us/eval.usoeeval.htm |
| Vermont | http://www.cit.state.vt.us/educ/ | http://www.fairtest.org/states/vt.htm |

| STATE | GENERAL WEB SITE | STATE TESTING WEB SITE |
|---|---|---|
| Virginia | http://www.pen.k12.va.us/Anthology/VDOE/ | http://www.pen.k12.va.us/VDOE/Assessment/home.shtml |
| Washington | http://www.k12.wa.us/ | http://assessment.ospi.wednet.edu/ |
| West Virginia | http://wvde.state.wv.us/ | http://www.fairtest.org/states/wv.htm |
| Wisconsin | http://www.dpi.state.wi.us/ | http://www.dpi.state.wi.us/dpi/oea/spr_kce.html |
| Wyoming | http://www.k12.wy.us/wdehome.html | http://www.asme.com/wycas/index.htm |

**Table 2**  Norm-Referenced and Criterion-Referenced Tests Administered by State

| STATE | NORM-REFERENCED TEST | CRITERION-REFERENCED TEST | EXIT EXAM |
|---|---|---|---|
| Alabama | Stanford Achievement Test | | Alabama High School Graduation Exam |
| Alaska | California Achievement Test | | |
| Arizona | Stanford Achievement Test | Arizona's Instrument to Measure Standards (AIMS) | |
| Arkansas | Stanford Achievement Test | | |
| California | Stanford Achievement Test | Standardized Testing and Reporting Supplement | High School Exit Exam (HSEE) |
| Colorado | None | Colorado Student Assessment Program | |
| Connecticut | | Connecticut Mastery Test | |
| Delaware | Stanford Achievement Test | Delaware Student Testing Program | |
| District of Columbia | Stanford Achievement Test | | |
| Florida | (Locally Selected) | Florida Comprehensive Assessment Test (FCAT) | High School Competency Test (HSCT) |
| Georgia | Iowa Tests of Basic Skills | Criterion-Referenced Competency Tests (CRCT) | Georgia High School Graduation Tests |
| Hawaii | Stanford Achievement Test | Credit by Examination | Hawaii State Test of Essential Competencies |
| Idaho | Iowa Test of Basic Skills/ Tests of Direct Achievement and Proficiency | Writing/Mathematics Assessment | |
| Illinois | | Illinois Standards Achievement Tests | Prairie State Achievement Examination |
| Indiana | | Indiana Statewide Testing for Education Progress | |
| Iowa | (None) | | |
| Kansas | | (State-Developed Tests) | |
| Kentucky | Comprehensive Tests of Basic Skills | Kentucky Instructional Results Information System | |
| Louisiana | Iowa Tests of Basic Skills | Louisiana Educational Assessment Program | Graduate Exit Exam |
| Maine | | Maine Educational Assessment | |
| Maryland | | Maryland School Performance Assessment Program | |
| Massachusetts | | Massachusetts Comprehensive Assessment System | |

| STATE | NORM-REFERENCED TEST | CRITERION-REFERENCED TEST | EXIT EXAM |
|---|---|---|---|
| Michigan | | Michigan Educational Assessment Program | High School Test |
| Minnesota | | Basic Standards Test | Profile of Learning |
| Mississippi | Iowa Test of Basic Skills | Subject Area Testing Program | Functional Literacy Examination |
| Missouri | | Missouri Mastery and Achievement Test | |
| Montana | (districts' choice) | | |
| Nebraska | | | |
| Nevada | TerraNova | | Nevada High School Proficiency Examination |
| New Hampshire | | NH Educational Improvement and Assessment Program | |
| New Jersey | | Elementary School Proficiency Test/Early Warning Test | High School Proficiency Test |
| New Mexico | TerraNova | | New Mexico High School Competency Exam |
| New York | | Pupil Evaluation Program/ Preliminary Competency Test | Regents Competency Tests |
| North Carolina | Iowa Test of Basic Skills | NC End of Grade Test | |
| North Dakota | TerraNova | ND Reading, Writing Speaking, Listening, Math Test | |
| Ohio | | Ohio Proficiency Tests | Ohio Proficiency Tests |
| Oklahoma | Iowa Tests of Basic Skills | Oklahoma Criterion-Referenced Tests | |
| Oregon | | Oregon Statewide Assessment | |
| Pennsylvania | | Pennsylvania System of School Assessment | |
| Rhode Island | Metropolitan Achievement Test | | |
| South Carolina | TerraNova | Palmetto Achievement Challenge Tests | High School Exit Exam |
| South Dakota | Stanford Achievement Test | | |
| Tennessee | Tennessee Comprehensive Assessment Program | Tennessee Comprehensive Assessment Program | |
| Texas | | Texas Assessment of Academic Skills | Texas Assessment of Academic Skills |
| Utah | Stanford Achievement Test | Core Curriculum Testing | |

| STATE | NORM-REFERENCED TEST | CRITERION-REFERENCED TEST | EXIT EXAM |
|---|---|---|---|
| Vermont | | New Standards Reference Exams | |
| Virginia | Stanford Achievement Test | Virginia Standards of Learning | Virginia Standards of Learning |
| Washington | Iowa Tests of Basic Skills | Washington Assessment of Student Learning | Washington Assessment of Student Learning |
| West Virginia | Stanford Achievement Test | | |
| Wisconsin | TerraNova | Wisconsin Knowledge and Concepts Examinations | |
| Wyoming | TerraNova | Wyoming Comprehensive Assessment System | Wyoming Comprehensive Assessment System |

**Table 3**   Standardized Test Schedules by State

| STATE | KG | 1 | 2 | 3 | 4 | 5 | 6 | 7 | 8 | 9 | 10 | 11 | 12 | COMMENT |
|---|---|---|---|---|---|---|---|---|---|---|---|---|---|---|
| Alabama | | | | X | X | X | X | X | X | X | X | X | X | |
| Alaska | | | | | X | | | | X | | | X | | |
| Arizona | | | X | X | X | X | X | X | X | X | X | X | X | |
| Arkansas | | | | | X | X | | X | X | | X | X | X | |
| California | | | X | X | X | X | X | X | X | X | X | X | | |
| Colorado | | | | X | X | | | X | | | | | | |
| Connecticut | | | | | X | | X | | X | | | | | |
| Delaware | | | | X | X | X | | X | | X | X | | | |
| District of Columbia | | X | X | X | X | X | X | X | X | X | X | X | | |
| Florida | | X | X | X | X | X | X | X | X | X | X | X | X | There is no state-mandated norm-referenced testing. However, the state collects information furnished by local districts that elect to perform norm-referenced testing. The FCAT is administered to Grades 4, 8, and 10 to assess reading and Grades 5, 8, and 10 to assess math. |
| Georgia | | | | X | | X | | | X | | | | | |
| Hawaii | | | | X | | | X | | X | | X | | | The Credit by Examination is voluntary and is given in Grade 8 in Algebra and Foreign Languages. |
| Idaho | | | | X | X | X | X | X | X | X | X | X | | |
| Illinois | | | | X | X | | X | X | X | | X | X | | Exit Exam failure will not disqualify students from graduation if all other requirements are met. |
| Indiana | | | | X | | | X | | X | | X | | | |
| Iowa | | * | * | * | * | * | * | * | * | * | * | * | * | *Iowa does not currently have a statewide testing program. Locally chosen assessments are administered to grades determined locally. |
| Kansas | | | | X | X | X | | X | X | | X | | | |

| STATE | KG | 1 | 2 | 3 | 4 | 5 | 6 | 7 | 8 | 9 | 10 | 11 | 12 | COMMENT |
|---|---|---|---|---|---|---|---|---|---|---|---|---|---|---|
| Kentucky | | | | | X | X | | X | X | | | X | X | |
| Louisiana | | | | X | | X | X | X | | X | | | | |
| Maine | | | | | X | | | | X | | | X | | |
| Maryland | | | | X | | X | | | X | | | | | |
| Massachusetts | | | | | X | | | | X | | X | | | |
| Michigan | | | | | X | X | | X | X | | | | | |
| Minnesota | | | | X | | X | | | X | | | | | Testing Information from Fair Test.Org. There was no readily accessible state-sponsored site. |
| Mississippi | | | | | X | X | X | X | X | | | | | State's Web site refused connection; all data were obtained from FairTest.Org. |
| Missouri | | | X | X | X | X | X | X | X | X | X | | | |
| Montana | | | | | X | | | | X | | | X | | The State Board of Education has decided to use a single norm-referenced test statewide beginning 2000–2001 school year. |
| Nebraska | | ** | ** | ** | ** | ** | ** | ** | ** | ** | ** | ** | ** | **Decisions regarding testing are left to the individual school districts. |
| Nevada | | | | | X | | | | X | | | | | Districts choose whether and how to test with norm-referenced tests. |
| New Hampshire | | | | X | | | X | | | | X | | | |
| New Jersey | | | | X | X | | | X | X | X | X | X | | |
| New Mexico | | | | | X | | X | | X | | | | | |
| New York | | | | | X | | | | X | X | | | | Assessment program is going through major revisions. |
| North Carolina | | | | X | X | X | X | X | X | | X | | | NRT Testing selects samples of students, not all. |
| North Dakota | | | | | X | | X | | X | | X | | | |
| Ohio | | | | | X | | X | | | X | | | X | |
| Oklahoma | | | | X | | X | | X | X | | | X | | |
| Oregon | | | | X | | X | | | X | | X | | | |

| STATE | KG | 1 | 2 | 3 | 4 | 5 | 6 | 7 | 8 | 9 | 10 | 11 | 12 | COMMENT |
|---|---|---|---|---|---|---|---|---|---|---|---|---|---|---|
| Pennsylvania |  |  |  |  |  | X | X |  | X | X |  | X |  |  |
| Rhode Island |  |  |  | X | X | X |  | X | X | X | X |  |  |  |
| South Carolina |  |  |  | X | X | X | X | X | X | X | X |  |  |  |
| South Dakota |  |  | X |  | X | X |  |  | X | X |  | X |  |  |
| Tennessee |  |  | X | X | X | X | X | X | X |  |  | X |  |  |
| Texas |  |  |  | X | X | X | X | X | X |  | X |  |  |  |
| Utah |  | X | X | X | X | X | X | X | X | X | X | X | X |  |
| Vermont |  |  |  |  | X | X | X |  | X | X | X | X |  |  | Rated by FairTest.Org as a nearly model system for assessment. |
| Virginia |  |  |  | X | X | X | X |  | X | X |  | X |  |  |
| Washington |  |  |  |  | X |  |  | X |  |  | X |  |  |  |
| West Virginia |  | X | X | X | X | X | X | X | X | X | X | X |  |  |
| Wisconsin |  |  |  |  | X |  |  |  | X |  | X |  |  |  |
| Wyoming |  |  |  |  | X |  |  |  | X |  |  | X |  |  |

# Testing Accommodations

The more testing procedures vary from one classroom or school to the next, the less we can compare the scores from one group to another. Consider a test in which the publisher recommends that three sections of the test be given in one 45-minute session per day on three consecutive days. School A follows those directions. To save time, School B gives all three sections of the test in one session lasting slightly more than two hours. We can't say that both schools followed the same testing procedures. Remember that the test publishers provide testing procedures so schools can administer the tests in as close a manner as possible to the way the tests were administered to the groups used to obtain test norms. When we compare students' scores to norms, we want to compare apples to apples, not apples to oranges.

Most schools justifiably resist making any changes in testing procedures. Informally, a teacher can make minor changes that don't alter the testing procedures, such as separating two students who talk with each other instead of paying attention to the test; letting Lisa, who is getting over an ear infection, sit closer to the front so she can hear better; or moving Jeffrey away from the window to prevent his looking out the window and daydreaming.

There are two groups of students who require more formal testing accommodations. One group of students is identified as having a disability under Section 504 of the Rehabilitation Act of 1973 (Public Law 93-112). These students face some challenge but, with reasonable and appropriate accommodation, can take advantage of the same educational opportunities as other students. That is, they have a condition that requires some accommodation for them.

Just as schools must remove physical barriers to accommodate students with disabilities, they must make appropriate accommodations to remove other types of barriers to students' access to education. Marie is profoundly deaf, even with strong hearing aids. She does well in school with the aid of an interpreter, who signs her teacher's instructions to her and tells her teacher what Marie says in reply. An appropriate accommodation for Marie would be to provide the interpreter to sign test instructions to her, or to allow her to watch a videotape with an interpreter signing test instructions. Such a reasonable accommodation would not deviate from standard testing procedures and, in fact, would ensure that Marie received the same instructions as the other students.

If your child is considered disabled and has what is generally called a Section 504 Plan or individual accommodation plan (IAP), then the appropriate way to ask for testing accommodations is to ask for them in a meeting to discuss school accommodations under the plan. If your child is not already covered by such a plan, he or she won't qualify for one merely because you request testing accommodations.

The other group of students who may receive formal testing accommodations are those identified as handicapped under the Individuals with Disabilities Education Act (IDEA)—students with mental retardation, learning disabilities, serious emotional disturbance, orthopedic handicap, hearing or visual problems, and other handicaps defined in the law. These students have been identified under procedures governed by federal and sometimes state law, and their education is governed by a document called the Individualized Educational Program (IEP). Unless you are under a court order specifically revoking your educational rights on behalf of your child, you are a full member of the IEP team even if you and your child's other parent are divorced and the other parent has custody. Until recently, IEP teams actually had the prerogative to exclude certain handicapped students from taking standardized group testing altogether. However, today states make it more difficult to exclude students from testing.

If your child is classified as handicapped and has an IEP, the appropriate place to ask for testing accommodations is in an IEP team meeting. In fact, federal regulations require IEP teams to address testing accommodations. You have the right to call a meeting at any time. In that meeting, you will have the opportunity to present your case for the accommodations you believe are necessary. Be prepared for the other team members to resist making extreme accommodations unless you can present a very strong case. If your child is identified as handicapped and you believe that he or she should be provided special testing accommodations, contact the person at your child's school who is responsible for convening IEP meetings and request a meeting to discuss testing accommodations.

Problems arise when a request is made for accommodations that cause major departures from standard testing procedures. For example, Lynn has an identified learning disability in mathematics calculation and attends resource classes for math. Her disability is so severe that her IEP calls for her to use a calculator when performing all math problems. She fully understands math concepts, but she simply can't perform the calculations without the aid of a calculator. Now it's time for Lynn to take the school-based standardized tests, and she asks to use a calculator. In this case, since her IEP already requires her to be provided with a calculator when performing math calculations, she may be allowed a calculator during school standardized tests. However, because using a calculator constitutes a major violation of standard testing procedures, her score on all sections in which she is allowed to use a calculator will be recorded as a failure, and her results in some states will be removed from among those of other students in her school in calculating school results.

How do we determine whether a student is allowed formal accommodations in standardized school testing and what these accommodations may be? First, if your child is not already identified as either handicapped or disabled, having the child classified in either group solely to receive testing accommodations will be considered a violation of the laws governing both classifications. Second, even if your child is already classified in either group, your state's department of public instruction will provide strict guidelines for the testing accommodations schools may make. Third, even if your child is classified in either group and you are proposing testing accommodations allowed under state testing guidelines, any accommodations must still be both *reasonable* and *appropriate*. To be reasonable and appropriate, testing accommodations must relate to your child's disability and must be similar to those already in place in his or her daily educational program. If your child is always tested individually in a separate room for all tests in all subjects, then a similar practice in taking school-based standardized tests may be appropriate. But if your child has a learning disability only in mathematics calculation, requesting that all test questions be read to him or her is inappropriate because that accommodation does not relate to his identified handicap.

# Glossary

**Accountability**   The idea that a school district is held responsible for the achievement of its students. The term may also be applied to holding students responsible for a certain level of achievement in order to be promoted or to graduate.

**Achievement test**   An assessment that measures current knowledge in one or more of the areas taught in most schools, such as reading, math, and language arts.

**Aptitude test**   An assessment designed to predict a student's potential for learning knowledge or skills.

**Content validity**   The extent to which a test represents the content it is designed to cover.

**Criterion-referenced test**   A test that rates how thoroughly a student has mastered a specific skill or area of knowledge. Typically, a criterion-referenced test is subjective, and relies on someone to observe and rate student work; it doesn't allow for easy comparisons of achievement among students. Performance assessments are criterion-referenced tests. The opposite of a criterion-referenced test is a norm-referenced test.

**Frequency distribution**   A tabulation of individual scores (or groups of scores) that shows the number of persons who obtained each score.

**Generalizability**   The idea that the score on a test reflects what a child knows about a subject, or how well he performs the skills the test is supposed to be assessing. Generalizability requires that enough test items are administered to truly assess a student's achievement.

**Grade equivalent**   A score on a scale developed to indicate the school grade (usually measured in months of a year) that corresponds to an average chronological age, mental age, test score, or other characteristic. A grade equivalent of 6.4 is interpreted as a score that is average for a group in the fourth month of Grade 6.

**High-stakes assessment**   A type of standardized test that has major consequences for a student or school (such as whether a child graduates from high school or gets admitted to college).

**Mean**   Average score of a group of scores.

**Median**   The middle score in a set of scores ranked from smallest to largest.

**National percentile**   Percentile score derived from the performance of a group of individuals across the nation.

**Normative sample**   A comparison group consisting of individuals who have taken a test under standard conditions.

**Norm-referenced test** A standardized test that can compare scores of students in one school with a reference group (usually other students in the same grade and age, called the "norm group"). Norm-referenced tests compare the achievement of one student or the students of a school, school district, or state with the norm score.

**Norms** A summary of the performance of a group of individuals on which a test was standardized.

**Percentile** An incorrect form of the word *centile,* which is the percent of a group of scores that falls below a given score. Although the correct term is *centile,* much of the testing literature has adopted the term *percentile.*

**Performance standards** A level of performance on a test set by education experts.

**Quartiles** Points that divide the frequency distribution of scores into equal fourths.

**Regression to the mean** The tendency of scores in a group of scores to vary in the direction of the mean. For example: If a child has an abnormally low score on a test, she is likely to make a higher score (that is, one closer to the mean) the next time she takes the test.

**Reliability** The consistency with which a test measures some trait or characteristic. A measure can be reliable without being valid, but it can't be valid without being reliable.

**Standard deviation** A statistical measure used to describe the extent to which scores vary in a group of scores. Approximately 68 percent of scores in a group are expected to be in a range from one standard deviation below the mean to one standard deviation above the mean.

**Standardized test** A test that contains well-defined questions of proven validity and that produces reliable scores. Such tests are commonly paper-and-pencil exams containing multiple-choice items, true or false questions, matching exercises, or short fill-in-the-blanks items. These tests may also include performance assessment items (such as a writing sample), but assessment items cannot be completed quickly or scored reliably.

**Test anxiety** Anxiety that occurs in test-taking situations. Test anxiety can seriously impair individuals' ability to obtain accurate scores on a test.

**Validity** The extent to which a test measures the trait or characteristic it is designed to measure. Also see *reliability.*

# Answer Keys for Practice Skills

**Chapter 2:**
**Vocabulary**

| | |
|---|---|
| 1 | B |
| 2 | D |
| 3 | A |
| 4 | C |
| 5 | C |
| 6 | D |
| 7 | A |
| 8 | C |
| 9 | B |
| 10 | C |
| 11 | D |
| 12 | A |
| 13 | B |
| 14 | C |
| 15 | B |
| 16 | B |
| 17 | A |
| 18 | A |
| 19 | B |
| 20 | A |
| 21 | B |
| 22 | C |
| 23 | D |
| 24 | D |
| 25 | A |
| 26 | B |
| 27 | D |
| 28 | D |
| 29 | C |

**Chapter 3:**
**Reading**
**Comprehension**

| | |
|---|---|
| 1 | C |
| 2 | D |
| 3 | C |
| 4 | C |
| 5 | A |
| 6 | B |
| 7 | B |
| 8 | A |
| 9 | C |
| 10 | B |
| 11 | C |
| 12 | A |
| 13 | D |
| 14 | D |
| 15 | A |

**Chapter 4:**
**Language Mechanics**

| | |
|---|---|
| 1 | A |
| 2 | C |
| 3 | B |
| 4 | B |
| 5 | B |
| 6 | B |
| 7 | B |
| 8 | D |
| 9 | C |
| 10 | D |

| | |
|---|---|
| 11 | B |
| 12 | A |
| 13 | B |

**Chapter 5:**
**Language Expression**

| | |
|---|---|
| 1 | A |
| 2 | A |
| 3 | C |
| 4 | A |
| 5 | B |
| 6 | B |
| 7 | C |
| 8 | B |
| 9 | D |
| 10 | B |
| 11 | D |
| 12 | B |
| 13 | D |
| 14 | A |
| 15 | C |
| 16 | B |

**Chapter 6:**
**Spelling and Study Skills**

| | |
|---|---|
| 1 | B |
| 2 | E |
| 3 | C |
| 4 | D |
| 5 | B |

| | |
|---|---|
| 6 | C |
| 7 | B |
| 8 | D |
| 9 | A |
| 10 | D |
| 11 | D |
| 12 | A |
| 13 | D |
| 14 | C |
| 15 | D |
| 16 | B |
| 17 | D |
| 18 | D |
| 19 | B |
| 20 | D |
| 21 | B |

**Chapter 7:**
**Math Concepts**

| | |
|---|---|
| 1 | B |
| 2 | C |
| 3 | D |
| 4 | D |
| 5 | D |
| 6 | B |
| 7 | C |
| 8 | C |
| 9 | B |
| 10 | A |
| 11 | A |
| 12 | D |

| | | | | | | | |
|---|---|---|---|---|---|---|---|
| 13 | B | 34 | A | 16 | B | 10 | D |
| 14 | C | 35 | D | 17 | D | 11 | B |
| 15 | C | 36 | A | 18 | B | 12 | A |
| 16 | D | | | 19 | D | 13 | C |
| 17 | A | | | 20 | A | 14 | D |
| 18 | B | | | 21 | C | 15 | C |
| 19 | A | | | 22 | B | 16 | B |
| 20 | C | | | 23 | E | 17 | D |
| 21 | B | | | 24 | D | 18 | D |
| 22 | D | | | | | 19 | A |
| 23 | A | | | | | 20 | C |
| 24 | B | | | | | 21 | B |
| 25 | C | | | | | 22 | D |
| 26 | D | | | | | 23 | C |
| 27 | C | | | | | 24 | A |
| 28 | A | | | | | 25 | D |
| 29 | A | | | | | 26 | C |
| 30 | D | | | | | 27 | D |
| 31 | C | | | | | 28 | C |
| 32 | B | | | | | 29 | A |
| 33 | C | | | | | 30 | B |

## Chapter 8: Math Computation

| | |
|---|---|
| 1 | B |
| 2 | D |
| 3 | A |
| 4 | D |
| 5 | E |
| 6 | A |
| 7 | C |
| 8 | B |
| 9 | D |
| 10 | D |
| 11 | A |
| 12 | E |
| 13 | B |
| 14 | B |
| 15 | D |

## Chapter 9: Math Applications

| | |
|---|---|
| 1 | B |
| 2 | D |
| 3 | C |
| 4 | A |
| 5 | D |
| 6 | C |
| 7 | B |
| 8 | A |
| 9 | D |

# Sample Practice Test

The test questions given here are designed to provide a sample of the kinds of items fifth-grade students may encounter on a standardized test. They are *not* identical to any standardized test your child will take. However, the questions cover all the areas discussed in this book and provide a review that is similar in format to a standardized test.

The sample test provides 116 questions organized by skill areas presented in the preceding chapters. It is intended to provide a rough idea about the types of test questions your child will probably encounter on the commercial standardized tests provided at school. It is not an exact copy.

## How to Use the Test

In this guide, we have been more concerned with strengthening certain skills than with the ability to work under time constraints. We don't recommend that you attempt to simulate actual testing conditions. Here are four alternative ways of using this test:

1. Administer these tests to your child after you have completed all skills chapters and have begun to implement the strategies we suggested. Allow your child to work at a leisurely pace, probably consisting of 20- to 30-minute sessions spread out over several days.

2. Administer the pertinent section of the test after you have been through each chapter and implemented the strategies.

3. Use the tests as a pretest rather than as a posttest, administering the entire test in 20- to 30-minute sessions spread out over several days to identify the skills on which your child needs the most work. Then concentrate most of your efforts on the skills on which your child scores the lowest.

4. Administer each section of the test before you go through each chapter as a kind of skills check to help you determine how much of your energy you need to devote to that skill area.

## Administering the Test

Don't provide any help to your child during these tests, but note specific problems. For example, if your child has problems reading math sentences, note whether the problem is with reading rather than with math. If your child's answers look sloppy, with many erasures or cross-outs, note that you need to work on neatness. (Remember that tests administered at school will be machine-scored, and the scanners sometimes mistake sloppily erased answers as the answers the child intends.)

## To the Student:

These tests will give you a chance to put the tips you have learned to work.

A few last reminders . . .

- Be sure you understand all the directions before you begin each test. You may ask the teacher questions about the directions if you do not understand them.

- Work as quickly as you can during each test.

- When you change an answer, be sure to erase your first mark completely.

- You can guess at an answer or skip difficult items and go back to them later.

- Use the tips you have learned whenever you can.

- It is OK to be a little nervous. You may even do better.

Now that you have completed the lessons in this book, you are on your way to scoring high!

Cut along dashed line.

| STUDENT'S NAME | | | SCHOOL |
|---|---|---|---|
| LAST | FIRST | MI | TEACHER |

FEMALE ○          MALE ○

**BIRTHDATE**

| MONTH | DAY | YEAR |
|---|---|---|

JAN ○
FEB ○
MAR ○
APR ○
MAY ○
JUN ○
JUL ○
AUG ○
SEP ○
OCT ○
NOV ○
DEC ○

**GRADE**

① ② ③ ④ ⑤ ⑥

## Vocabulary

1 Ⓐ Ⓑ Ⓒ Ⓓ   4 Ⓐ Ⓑ Ⓒ Ⓓ   7 Ⓐ Ⓑ Ⓒ Ⓓ   10 Ⓐ Ⓑ Ⓒ Ⓓ   13 Ⓐ Ⓑ Ⓒ Ⓓ
2 Ⓐ Ⓑ Ⓒ Ⓓ   5 Ⓐ Ⓑ Ⓒ Ⓓ   8 Ⓐ Ⓑ Ⓒ Ⓓ   11 Ⓐ Ⓑ Ⓒ Ⓓ   14 Ⓐ Ⓑ Ⓒ Ⓓ
3 Ⓐ Ⓑ Ⓒ Ⓓ   6 Ⓐ Ⓑ Ⓒ Ⓓ   9 Ⓐ Ⓑ Ⓒ Ⓓ   12 Ⓐ Ⓑ Ⓒ Ⓓ

## Reading Comprehension

1 Ⓐ Ⓑ Ⓒ Ⓓ   4 Ⓐ Ⓑ Ⓒ Ⓓ   7 Ⓐ Ⓑ Ⓒ Ⓓ   10 Ⓐ Ⓑ Ⓒ Ⓓ   13 Ⓐ Ⓑ Ⓒ Ⓓ
2 Ⓐ Ⓑ Ⓒ Ⓓ   5 Ⓐ Ⓑ Ⓒ Ⓓ   8 Ⓐ Ⓑ Ⓒ Ⓓ   11 Ⓐ Ⓑ Ⓒ Ⓓ   14 Ⓐ Ⓑ Ⓒ Ⓓ
3 Ⓐ Ⓑ Ⓒ Ⓓ   6 Ⓐ Ⓑ Ⓒ Ⓓ   9 Ⓐ Ⓑ Ⓒ Ⓓ   12 Ⓐ Ⓑ Ⓒ Ⓓ

## Language Mechanics

1 Ⓐ Ⓑ Ⓒ Ⓓ   4 Ⓐ Ⓑ Ⓒ Ⓓ   7 Ⓐ Ⓑ Ⓒ Ⓓ   10 Ⓐ Ⓑ Ⓒ Ⓓ   12 Ⓐ Ⓑ Ⓒ Ⓓ
2 Ⓐ Ⓑ Ⓒ Ⓓ   5 Ⓐ Ⓑ Ⓒ Ⓓ   8 Ⓐ Ⓑ Ⓒ Ⓓ   11 Ⓐ Ⓑ Ⓒ Ⓓ
3 Ⓐ Ⓑ Ⓒ Ⓓ   6 Ⓐ Ⓑ Ⓒ Ⓓ   9 Ⓐ Ⓑ Ⓒ Ⓓ

## Language Expression

1 Ⓐ Ⓑ Ⓒ Ⓓ   5 Ⓐ Ⓑ Ⓒ Ⓓ   8 Ⓐ Ⓑ Ⓒ Ⓓ   11 Ⓐ Ⓑ Ⓒ Ⓓ   14 Ⓐ Ⓑ Ⓒ Ⓓ
2 Ⓐ Ⓑ Ⓒ Ⓓ   6 Ⓐ Ⓑ Ⓒ Ⓓ   9 Ⓐ Ⓑ Ⓒ Ⓓ   12 Ⓐ Ⓑ Ⓒ Ⓓ   15 Ⓐ Ⓑ Ⓒ Ⓓ
3 Ⓐ Ⓑ Ⓒ Ⓓ   7 Ⓐ Ⓑ Ⓒ Ⓓ   10 Ⓐ Ⓑ Ⓒ Ⓓ   13 Ⓐ Ⓑ Ⓒ Ⓓ   16 Ⓐ Ⓑ Ⓒ Ⓓ
4 Ⓐ Ⓑ Ⓒ Ⓓ

## Spelling

1 Ⓐ Ⓑ Ⓒ Ⓓ   3 Ⓐ Ⓑ Ⓒ Ⓓ   5 Ⓐ Ⓑ Ⓒ Ⓓ   7 Ⓐ Ⓑ Ⓒ Ⓓ   8 Ⓐ Ⓑ Ⓒ Ⓓ
2 Ⓐ Ⓑ Ⓒ Ⓓ   4 Ⓐ Ⓑ Ⓒ Ⓓ   6 Ⓐ Ⓑ Ⓒ Ⓓ

## Study Skills

1 Ⓐ Ⓑ Ⓒ Ⓓ   4 Ⓐ Ⓑ Ⓒ Ⓓ   7 Ⓐ Ⓑ Ⓒ Ⓓ   10 Ⓐ Ⓑ Ⓒ Ⓓ   12 Ⓐ Ⓑ Ⓒ Ⓓ
2 Ⓐ Ⓑ Ⓒ Ⓓ   5 Ⓐ Ⓑ Ⓒ Ⓓ   8 Ⓐ Ⓑ Ⓒ Ⓓ   11 Ⓐ Ⓑ Ⓒ Ⓓ
3 Ⓐ Ⓑ Ⓒ Ⓓ   6 Ⓐ Ⓑ Ⓒ Ⓓ   9 Ⓐ Ⓑ Ⓒ Ⓓ

## Math Concepts

1 Ⓐ Ⓑ Ⓒ Ⓓ   6 Ⓐ Ⓑ Ⓒ Ⓓ   11 Ⓐ Ⓑ Ⓒ Ⓓ   16 Ⓐ Ⓑ Ⓒ Ⓓ   20 Ⓐ Ⓑ Ⓒ Ⓓ
2 Ⓐ Ⓑ Ⓒ Ⓓ   7 Ⓐ Ⓑ Ⓒ Ⓓ   12 Ⓐ Ⓑ Ⓒ Ⓓ   17 Ⓐ Ⓑ Ⓒ Ⓓ   21 Ⓐ Ⓑ Ⓒ Ⓓ
3 Ⓐ Ⓑ Ⓒ Ⓓ   8 Ⓐ Ⓑ Ⓒ Ⓓ   13 Ⓐ Ⓑ Ⓒ Ⓓ   18 Ⓐ Ⓑ Ⓒ Ⓓ
4 Ⓐ Ⓑ Ⓒ Ⓓ   9 Ⓐ Ⓑ Ⓒ Ⓓ   14 Ⓐ Ⓑ Ⓒ Ⓓ   19 Ⓐ Ⓑ Ⓒ Ⓓ
5 Ⓐ Ⓑ Ⓒ Ⓓ   10 Ⓐ Ⓑ Ⓒ Ⓓ   15 Ⓐ Ⓑ Ⓒ Ⓓ

## Math Computation

1 Ⓐ Ⓑ Ⓒ Ⓓ   5 Ⓐ Ⓑ Ⓒ Ⓓ   9 Ⓐ Ⓑ Ⓒ Ⓓ   13 Ⓐ Ⓑ Ⓒ Ⓓ   17 Ⓐ Ⓑ Ⓒ Ⓓ
2 Ⓐ Ⓑ Ⓒ Ⓓ   6 Ⓐ Ⓑ Ⓒ Ⓓ   10 Ⓐ Ⓑ Ⓒ Ⓓ   14 Ⓐ Ⓑ Ⓒ Ⓓ   18 Ⓐ Ⓑ Ⓒ Ⓓ
3 Ⓐ Ⓑ Ⓒ Ⓓ   7 Ⓐ Ⓑ Ⓒ Ⓓ   11 Ⓐ Ⓑ Ⓒ Ⓓ   15 Ⓐ Ⓑ Ⓒ Ⓓ   19 Ⓐ Ⓑ Ⓒ Ⓓ
4 Ⓐ Ⓑ Ⓒ Ⓓ   8 Ⓐ Ⓑ Ⓒ Ⓓ   12 Ⓐ Ⓑ Ⓒ Ⓓ   16 Ⓐ Ⓑ Ⓒ Ⓓ

Cut along dashed line.

# VOCABULARY

**Directions:** Read each question carefully and choose the correct answer.

**1** Which word is a synonym of the underlined word?

He used a lot of <u>gestures</u> when speaking.

**A** acts
**B** movements
**C** glances
**D** postures

**2** Which word is an antonym of the underlined word?

A <u>fierce</u> character

**A** savage
**B** strong
**C** hopeless
**D** meek

**3** Choose the word that correctly completes both sentences.

Mom put the serving of broccoli on my _____.

The umpire swept off home _____.

**A** dish
**B** base
**C** tray
**D** plate

**4** Choose the word that correctly completes both sentences.

No one can _____ you to think.

Gravity is a powerful _____.

**A** help
**B** weapon
**C** force
**D** weight

**5** Which answer best defines the underlined part of these words?

<u>Inter</u>national          <u>inter</u>change

**A** between
**B** under
**C** again
**D** opposing

**6** Which answer best defines the underlined part of these words?

Photo<u>graph</u>          Auto<u>graph</u>

**A** a machine
**B** a book
**C** something written or recorded
**D** a picture

Cut along dashed line.

**7** Which of these words probably came from the Greek word *glyphe* for <u>carving</u>?

   **A**   hieroglyphic
   **B**   glycerin
   **C**   glide
   **D**   glycol

**8** Which of these words probably came from the Latin word *liber* for <u>free</u>?

   **A**   liberal
   **B**   library
   **C**   libel
   **D**   liberty

**9** My mother loves to <u>direct</u> singers in a choir.

In which sentence does the word <u>direct</u> mean the same as in the sentence above?

   **A**   This is a <u>direct</u> flight from Atlanta to Boston.

   **B**   That policeman can <u>direct</u> traffic well.

   **C**   Please speak in a <u>direct</u> manner.

   **D**   This is a <u>direct</u> quote from the book.

**10** I <u>long</u> for summer vacation.

In which sentence does the word <u>long</u> mean the same as in the sentence above?

   **A**   *Anna and the King* is a <u>long</u> movie.

   **B**   The word <u>make</u> contains the long vowel sound of *a*.

   **C**   The seniors <u>long</u> for graduation from high school.

   **D**   How <u>long</u> do you need to finish this homework?

**Directions:** Read the paragraph. Find the word below the paragraph that fits best in each numbered blank.

Sharon needed to get a passport for her trip to Africa. She went to the Passport Office and took all her ___(11)___. The clerk acted very ___(12)___ and did not pay attention to her work. When Sharon did not receive her new passport in a ___(13)___ amount of time, she called the Passport Office. Imagine her ___(14)___ when she learned that all her papers had been lost!

**11**  **A**   documents
     **B**   suitcases
     **C**   clothes
     **D**   charge cards

**12**  **A**   kind
     **B**   pleasant
     **C**   greedy
     **D**   hurried

**13**  **A**   long
     **B**   reasonable
     **C**   quick
     **D**   short

**14**  **A**   happiness
     **B**   joyousness
     **C**   disappointment
     **D**   sorrow

Cut along dashed line.

**STOP**

# READING COMPREHENSION

**Directions:** Read this story about a girl's summer vacations in the 1950s and answer the questions following the story.

## The M & P Motel

When we were children, we spent every summer at our grandparents' house in a small town in West Virginia. All during the school year, we looked forward to those golden days at the M & P Motel, which was what we called their home. When my oldest cousin was a baby, she couldn't pronounce "Grandma" or "Grandpa," and so she shortened the names to "Ma" and "Pa." The names stuck for 17 more grandchildren, and so did the name of the M & P Motel. I've traveled around the world and I've never found a better motel in all my years of searching.

Frantic activity led up to our departure for the M & P. Our mothers had to buy play clothes and church clothes for all of us. We needed new shoes and new bathing suits. We had our hair cut and stocked up on comic books for the long trip. We packed a favorite stuffed animal—mine was named Kaplowie, a fine name for a little white poodle. My brother once had to leave his genuine Buffalo Bill toy rifle behind because it was too long to fit in the suitcase.

At last the big day arrived. We traveled to the M & P by different means, depending on where we lived. Sometimes we took a long car trip, sometimes we went on a Greyhound bus, sometimes we traveled by sleeper car on the train, and once we even flew in an airplane! Since the M & P was located in a small town tucked into the isolated glens of West Virginia, we usually had to travel to a large city like Pittsburgh or Washington, D.C., where our beloved grandfather Pa would meet us.

Pa was a Welsh coal miner. He loved children, jokes, music, family meals, and good times. His eyes were always twinkling. I always wondered if he was really Santa Claus in disguise. He would pile us children in the back of his big Hudson automobile and take off, tearing around the mountain curves on narrow, twisting highways like a man running for his life. To keep us amused, he would lead us in song. The children sang the melody and he and his daughters would harmonize. He knew all the favorites, like "Show Me the Way to Go Home" and "Down by the Old Mill Stream," and when he led us in "Drink to Me Only with Thine Eyes," the voices were so sweet and sincere that even Old Scrooge would have dropped a tear.

There was a courthouse in the center of our town with a big white dome. When we were close to the end of the trip, Pa would announce: "First one to see the courthouse gets a quarter!" A quarter! A huge sum for us children—enough to buy a comic book, five ice cream cones, or a day's supply of bubble gum. So the car grew silent while every eye was riveted on the horizon. When the first voice was raised, everyone would begin shouting, "I see it! I see it! There's the courthouse!" Pa would laugh merrily, stating that he knew exactly who had shouted first, and announce that the quarter would be dispensed when we got to the M & P. Strangely, each grubby fist ended up holding a shiny silver coin.

The M & P was a large brick three-story house with porches and cupolas and balconies. We children slept up on the third floor, which was really a large attic room filled with mismatched beds. We called it "The Dormitory"— our private domain, since parents rarely ascended those stairs. I remember one memorable evening in the old Dormitory. Most of us were in our beds with the lights out, doing what we did every evening: telling ghost stories. The older girls would add scary details to tales we'd learned at slumber parties back home so that we could frighten our little brothers and sisters. Everyone would shiver and scream, but we all loved being scared.

In the middle of one ghost story, we heard the door at the foot of the stairs creak open. We were instantly silent, afraid that a parent was listening to be sure we were all sleeping. But instead of a stern voice, we heard a muffled step on the bottom stair.

"Who's there?" one of us managed to call out weakly.

No answer; just another step and then another. Then a sickly light appeared on the ceiling over the stairwell and a dark shadow began to writhe on the wall. We watched in horror as the shadow grew larger. We were too scared to scream and just hugged each other in fright and prepared for the worst. Suddenly, a white form exploded over the banister! We shrieked in terror and began throwing our pillows at the thing to save ourselves. The creature threw up its arms to ward off the pillows, accidentally lifting the sheet too high. There were our three boy cousins, laughing so hard they could hardly stand. The enraged victims could scarcely believe their eyes. "I'll get even with you, Dusty Evans!" I screeched, looking for a book to throw at the fleeing boys.

**1** The setting for this story was:

- **A** a college dormitory
- **B** a slumber party
- **C** a small town in the mountains
- **D** a courthouse

**2** What do you predict the narrator would do at the end of the story?

- **A** Go to sleep.
- **B** Cry and hug her little cousins.
- **C** Tell her mother.
- **D** Plan a trick to play on Dusty.

**3** What do you think the author meant when she said that "Old Scrooge would have dropped a tear"?

- **A** The song was so sweet that even a bully would cry.
- **B** The song was so sweet that Mr. Scrooge might fall down.
- **C** The song was so sweet that a kind person would surely cry.
- **D** The song was so sweet that Mr. Scrooge might have an accident.

**4** What type of stuffed animal was Kaplowie?

- **A** a pig
- **B** a cat
- **C** a dog
- **D** a bear

**5** What is the tone of the final paragraph?

- **A** comedy
- **B** bitter
- **C** suspense
- **D** humor

**6** This story is an example of:

- **A** nonfiction
- **B** autobiography
- **C** science fiction
- **D** fantasy

**7** Judging from the information in this story, how much did ice cream cones cost in the 1950s?

- **A** a nickel
- **B** a quarter
- **C** a dime
- **D** two nickels

Cut along dashed line.

GO

**Directions:** Read this story about Norman Rockwell and answer the questions following the story.

## Norman Rockwell

Norman Rockwell is probably the most beloved illustrator in the world of American artists. He was born in 1894 in New York City and died in 1978 in Stockbridge, Massachusetts. During his long life as an artist, he painted hundreds of illustrations for magazines and books, many of which have been lost. He is chiefly remembered for his magazine covers for the *Saturday Evening Post,* a very popular weekly publication that was widely circulated in the United States.

Rockwell was a tall, skinny, and not very well-coordinated child who loved sports, but who wasn't very athletic. His true talent was drawing. By the time he was 18, he was already working as the art editor of *Boys' Life,* the official magazine of the Boy Scouts of America. He also illustrated children's books and submitted illustrations to other magazines that were popular in the early twentieth century. These paintings highlighted Americans in everyday situations: boys turning cartwheels, children returning to school, girls holding bouquets of spring flowers.

When Rockwell was 21, one of his illustrations was accepted for the cover of the *Saturday Evening Post.* His painting was a huge success, and Rockwell went on to illustrate 324 covers for that magazine alone. The magazine contained news of the day and articles by important writers. Since it was published every week, there were strict deadlines for the drawings and articles. Rockwell never missed a deadline, even though his canvases had to be sent from Arlington, Vermont to Philadelphia, Pennsylvania and often arrived with the oil paint still wet!

An illustrator is an artist who makes drawings that are designed to be inserted into written text as a way of helping to explain the text.

Rockwell often illustrated scenes from books for children and adults, but his famous covers for the *Saturday Evening Post* were actually illustrations of the lives of ordinary people in small towns in America. There are drawings of people at a barbershop, of parents sending their children off to college, of doctors examining children, and of neighbors gossiping. Rockwell often used his own friends, neighbors, and family members to people his scenes.

One of the most famous of Rockwell's paintings is called *Golden Rule.* As Rockwell recalled later, he got the idea that he should illustrate the Golden Rule, which is a quotation from the Bible: "Do unto others as you would have them do unto you." Rockwell was very excited about this idea and began thinking of a good way to illustrate the famous quotation. He remembered that he had an unfinished charcoal drawing in his cellar that he had begun as a drawing for the United Nations. The sketch was ten feet long, but Rockwell dragged it upstairs to his studio and got right to work. It took Rockwell five months to get the drawing right, but he was immensely pleased with his final product.

*Golden Rule* shows 28 men, women, and children from all over the world. The words of the quotation are drawn over the figures in gleaming golden letters outlined in black to make them seem embossed, or raised up from the canvas. The people represent different races and ethnic groups. They are wearing different costumes native to the group they represent. All the people seem serious and solemn. Rockwell was very pleased that he was able to use photos of his friends and neighbors from Vermont and Massachusetts as models for the figures. The old Jewish rabbi in the center of the painting was actually the Catholic postmaster of Rockwell's town. But it pleased the artist that there were descendants of so many immigrants living together in his town, a typical American village.

Rockwell won the Interfaith Award from the National Conference of Christians and

Jews for this striking work of art. He wanted to illustrate the idea that all men and women are members of the human family who are capable of living together in peace and harmony. Rockwell hoped that his paintings would contribute something positive to humanity. Most people who have been lucky enough to see this painting would agree that Rockwell achieved his goal.

**8** Most people probably became familiar with Rockwell's art by

   **A**   visiting museums
   **B**   reading Boy Scout magazines
   **C**   visiting his studio
   **D**   reading the *Saturday Evening Post*

**9** Another word for <u>cellar</u> is

   **A**   studio
   **B**   attic
   **C**   basement
   **D**   closet

**10** Where did Rockwell get the models for his paintings?

   **A**   He used photos of people from all over the world.

   **B**   He had people come to his studio to try out for the position.

   **C**   He worked from his memory and imagination.

   **D**   He used people from his town.

**11** Why do you think that some of the canvases arrived still wet in Philadelphia?

   **A**   Rockwell thought the glistening paint looked better.

   **B**   Rockwell was working on the drawing right up until the last minute.

   **C**   Rockwell never took time to let his paintings dry.

   **D**   The answer is not in the selection.

**12** Where did Rockwell get the quote used in his painting, *Golden Rule*?

   **A**   From a book
   **B**   From the Bible
   **C**   From another painting
   **D**   From his imagination

**13** Rockwell made the letters in *Golden Rule* appear raised or embossed by

   **A**   outlining them in black paint
   **B**   using a thicker layer of paint
   **C**   actually embossing the letters
   **D**   outlining them in gold paint

**14** One of Rockwell's goals was

   **A**   to become a great artist
   **B**   to become a sports star
   **C**   to paint covers for the *Saturday Evening Post*
   **D**   to make a positive contribution to humanity

Cut along dashed line.

STOP

# LANGUAGE MECHANICS

**Directions:** Read this report and use it to answer questions 1–6. The numbers in parentheses show which sentence is being indicated.

(1) Most people who live in and around new york city use public transportation To get to work? (2) Trains run into the city from new jersey connecticut and long island. (3) From Monday through Friday numerous trains collect riders between the hours of 6 and 9 in the Morning. (4) Since this system works well why haven't other cities followed this example.

1   In sentence 1, <u>new york city</u> is best written:

   **A**  New york city
   **B**  New York City
   **C**  New york City
   **D**  correct as it is

2   The punctuation mark that should go at the end of sentence 1 is:

   **A**  a period
   **B**  a question mark
   **C**  a comma
   **D**  an exclamation mark

3   The phrase from sentence 2 is best written:

   **A**  New Jersey Connecticut and Long Island
   **B**  New Jersey Connecticut, and Long Island
   **C**  New Jersey, Connecticut, and Long Island
   **D**  New Jersey, Connecticut, and long island

4   In sentence 3, the first phrase is best written

   **A**  From Monday through Friday
   **B**  From Monday through friday
   **C**  From monday through Friday
   **D**  From Monday through Friday,

5   The punctuation mark that should go at the end of sentence 4 is

   **A**  an exclamation mark
   **B**  a period
   **C**  a question mark
   **D**  a colon

6   There are two words in the paragraph that should not be capitalized. They are:

   **A**  To and Morning
   **B**  To and Since
   **C**  Trains and Morning
   **D**  Most and From

**Directions:** Mark the answer that shows the correct punctuation and capitalization.

7   <u>Julies</u> house is beautifully decorated.

   **A**  Julies'
   **B**  Julie's
   **C**  julie's
   **D**  correct as it is

8   At the day care center, the <u>babies'</u> room is very colorful.

   **A**  baby's
   **B**  babys'
   **C**  babie's
   **D**  correct as it is

Cut along dashed line.

**9** Heath <u>asked "why</u> do I have to go to school?"

    **A**    asked, "Why

    **B**    asked "Why

    **C**    asked, "why

    **D**    correct as it is

**10** "I don't know why my cable doesn't <u>work"</u> <u>said</u> April.

    **A**    work?" said

    **B**    work." said

    **C**    work," said

    **D**    correct as it is

**11** Stephanie's plane lands at <u>3:00 am.</u>

    **A**    3:00 A.M.

    **B**    correct as written

    **C**    3:00 Am.

    **D**    3:00 AM

**12** My father fought in <u>World War II.</u>

    **A**    world war II

    **B**    World war II

    **C**    world War II

    **D**    correct as it is

STOP

# LANGUAGE EXPRESSION

**Directions:** Choose the word that best completes the sentence.

**1** The winners were awarded _____ medals by the judges.

    **A** there
    **B** their
    **C** his
    **D** our

**2** This secret is just between you and _____.

    **A** I
    **B** he
    **C** she
    **D** me

**3** _____ supposed to report to the principal's office.

    **A** You're
    **B** Your
    **C** your
    **D** you're

**4** I am pleased because Jenny and Dave will be coming with us _____.

    **A** to
    **B** two
    **C** too
    **D** not given

**5** During elementary school, Kassie _____ her lunchbox to school.

    **A** brang
    **B** brought
    **C** brung
    **D** has brung

**6** The students injured _____ in a car accident.

    **A** theirselves
    **B** theirselfs
    **C** themselves
    **D** themself

**Directions:** For questions 7–9, choose the answer that best combines the underlined sentences.

**7** <u>We went to the grocery store yesterday.</u>

  <u>We needed to buy some cookies and apples at the grocery store.</u>

    **A** We went to the grocery store yesterday because we needed to buy some cookies and apples at the grocery store.

    **B** We went to the grocery store yesterday; however, we needed to buy some cookies and apples at the grocery store.

    **C** Because we needed to buy some cookies and apples, we went to the grocery store yesterday.

    **D** Yesterday we went to the grocery store because we needed to buy some cookies and apples.

**8**   My grandmother lived to be 108.

My grandmother enjoyed writing poetry.

My grandmother enjoyed painting flowers.

   **A**   My grandmother, who lived to be 108, enjoyed writing poetry and painting flowers.

   **B**   My grandmother lived to be 108 and she enjoyed writing poetry and she enjoyed painting flowers.

   **C**   My grandmother lived to be 108, enjoying writing poetry and painting flowers.

   **D**   My grandmother lived to be 108, because she enjoyed writing poetry and painting flowers.

**9**   Kay gives piano lessons to many children.

Kay doesn't like to listen to mistakes.

   **A**   Kay gives piano lessons to many children and she doesn't like to listen to mistakes.

   **B**   Kay gives piano lessons to many children because she doesn't like to listen to mistakes.

   **C**   Kay gives piano lessons to many children; she doesn't like to listen to mistakes.

   **D**   Kay gives piano lessons to many children, but she doesn't like to listen to mistakes.

**Directions:** For questions 10–12, choose the answer that is a complete and correctly written sentence.

**10**   **A**   This book don't be making no sense.
        **B**   This book makes no sense.
        **C**   This book don't make no sense.
        **D**   This book don't make any sense.

**11**   **A**   Do Scout be a girl?
        **B**   Are Scout a girl?
        **C**   Is Scout a girl?
        **D**   Do Scout be called a girl?

**12**   **A**   Arnold is the most tallest in his class.
        **B**   Tim is the most successful in his family.
        **C**   Brian is the more happier father.
        **D**   Nick has the more mileage on his car.

**Directions:** For questions 13–16, read the phrases and choose the phrase in which the underlined word is spelled correctly.

**13**   **A**   ate potatos
        **B**   saw two mouses
        **C**   found four pennys
        **D**   visited many countries

**14**   **A**   vacationed in the mountins
        **B**   an importint position
        **C**   deeply held beliefs
        **D**   a talented cheif

**15**   **A**   the leafy green vegtable
        **B**   the hevy weight
        **C**   discribe the stranger
        **D**   the exclusive restaurant

**16**   **A**   the oldest daughter
        **B**   my best freind
        **C**   gained much knowlege
        **D**   enjoyed sucess

STOP

# S P E L L I N G

**Directions:** For questions 1–3, mark the word that is spelled incorrectly.

1  **A**  ceeling
   **B**  receive
   **C**  believe
   **D**  seize

2  **A**  freight
   **B**  hight
   **C**  eight
   **D**  piece

3  **A**  hopeless
   **B**  happiness
   **C**  dropped
   **D**  swiming

**Directions:** In questions 4–8, one of the under-lined words is not spelled correctly for the way in which it is used in the phrase. Find the phrase with the incorrectly spelled word.

4  **A**  the <u>heel</u> of my foot
   **B**  the <u>ceiling</u> of my room
   **C**  the days of the <u>weak</u>
   **D**  <u>threw</u> the ball

5  **A**  the <u>principal</u> of the school
   **B**  the <u>plain</u> flew overhead
   **C**  the dress is too <u>loose</u>
   **D**  <u>hear</u> the birds chirping

6  **A**  the <u>coarse</u> sandpaper
   **B**  the sandy <u>dessert</u>
   **C**  the <u>altar</u> in front of the church
   **D**  to <u>break</u> a vase

7  **A**  the <u>too</u> sisters
   **B**  a <u>piece</u> of pie
   **C**  the <u>red</u> dress
   **D**  to <u>read</u> the line

8  **A**  the sun <u>shone</u>
   **B**  to speak in a <u>quite</u> voice
   **C**  look at the store over <u>there</u>
   **D**  to go <u>through</u> the door

STOP

# STUDY SKILLS

**Directions:** Use the Table of Contents and Index below to answer questions 1–4.

**Index**

Filleting, 28
Fishing Rigs
    Bottom fishing, 46–47
    Live bait rigs, 51–52
    Plastic worm rigs, 54–55
Hooks, 58–59
Knots
    Albright knot, 30
    Clinch knot, 31
    Turtle knot, 32
Locations
    Lakes, 98
    Ponds, 99
    Rivers, 100
    Streams, 101

**Table of Contents**

| Chapter | | Page |
|---|---|---|
| 1 | How to Fish | 1 |
| 2 | Fishing Techniques | 27 |
| 3 | Fishing Equipment | 45 |
| 4 | Lure Making | 62 |
| 5 | Fly Tying | 84 |
| 6 | Where to Fish | 98 |
| 7 | When to Fish | 114 |
| 8 | Fish Identification | 127 |

**1** Look at the Table of Contents. Which chapter might tell you how to tell a Coho salmon from a Chinook salmon?

- **A** Chapter 8
- **B** Chapter 2
- **C** Chapter 5
- **D** This information is not in the book.

**2** Look at the Index. Which page(s) would probably tell about how to fish on the Colorado River?

  **A** 98       **B** 101       **C** 28       **D** 100

**3** Look at the Table of Contents. Which chapter would be important if you wanted to know whether to plan your fishing trip for the early morning or late evening?

  **A** Chapter 2       **B** Chapter 6       **C** Chapter 7       **D** Chapter 4

**4** Look at the Index. What page(s) might tell you how to tie a lure onto the fish line?

  **A** 46–47       **B** 30–32       **C** 28       **D** 51–52

Cut along dashed line.

**GO**

Cut along dashed line.

**Directions:** For questions 5–7, choose the word that would appear first if the words were arranged in alphabetical order.

**5**  **A**  strain
    **B**  string
    **C**  straight
    **D**  strange

**6**  **A**  fragrant
    **B**  freeze
    **C**  fright
    **D**  frame

**7**  **A**  dream
    **B**  drown
    **C**  dress
    **D**  dragon

**Directions:** You are writing a report on the dangers of smoking. Answer questions 8–10 about your research for the paper.

**8**  You found a book titled *Nicotine Addiction.* Where would you look to get an overall picture of what is covered in the book?

    **A**  the glossary
    **B**  the index
    **C**  any of the pages
    **D**  the table of contents

**9**  Which topics would you not include in your report?

    **A**  How smoking increases the risk of lung cancer

    **B**  How smoking can make teens feel relaxed

    **C**  How smoking can interfere with exercise

    **D**  How smoking can increase chances of developing breathing problems

**10**  Which is a resource you might *not* use to get more information about smoking risks?

    **A**  the Internet
    **B**  the library
    **C**  the dictionary
    **D**  an encyclopedia

**Directions:** For questions 11 and 12, choose the best source of information.

**11**  Which of these would help you find a city in Iowa?

    **A**  an atlas
    **B**  a dictionary
    **C**  an encyclopedia
    **D**  a glossary

**12**  Which of these would help you find the year when George Washington died?

    **A**  a dictionary
    **B**  an encyclopedia
    **C**  an atlas
    **D**  a thesaurus

**STOP**

# MATH CONCEPTS

**Directions:** Read and work each problem. Mark the correct answer.

**1** 49 can be written as:

  **A** $2^7$
  **B** $9^4$
  **C** $4^9$
  **D** $7^2$

**2** Which two numbers are both factors of 36?

  **A** 3 and 7
  **B** 2 and 17
  **C** 1 and 7
  **D** 2 and 6

**3** Which of these numbers will have a remainder when it is divided by 7?

  **A** 49
  **B** 35
  **C** 58
  **D** 63

**4** Which of these numbers will have a remainder when it is divided by 5?

  **A** 25
  **B** 40
  **C** 63
  **D** 20

**5** Which of these numbers is between 0.90 and 1.5 in value?

  **A** 0.9
  **B** 1.00
  **C** 1.51
  **D** 0.89

**6** What number is expressed by:

| $(1 \times 1000) + (0 \times 100) + (0 \times 10) + (1 \times 1)$ |
| --- |

  **A** 1001
  **B** 1011
  **C** 1100
  **D** 1101

**7** $\sqrt{16}$ = _____

  **A** 2
  **B** 3
  **C** 4
  **D** 8

**8** What is another name for the Roman numeral L?

  **A** 50
  **B** 100
  **C** 500
  **D** 15

**9** How many of these numbers are common multiples of 3 and 6?

| 18 | 24 | 30 | 36 | 42 |
| --- | --- | --- | --- | --- |

  **A** 3
  **B** 5
  **C** 2
  **D** 4

**10** Which of these is both an odd number and a multiple of 5?

  **A** 17      **B** 35

  **C** 30      **D** 37

GO

**11** Which is the numeral for ten thousand, eight hundred seventy-nine?

   **A**   10,879
   **B**   1879
   **C**   100,879
   **D**   not given

---

**12** What rule would you use to find the number that is missing from the pattern below?

$$16, 12, 8, \underline{\quad}, 0$$

   **A**   Add 4 to each number to find the next number.

   **B**   Multiply each number by 4 to find the next number.

   **C**   Subtract 4 from each number to find the next number.

   **D**   Divide each number by 4 to find the next number.

---

**13** Which number makes all the number sentences below true?

$$16 \div \square = 4$$
$$\square \times 8 = 32$$
$$16 + \square \ 20$$
$$\square \times \square = 16$$

   **A**   2
   **B**   8
   **C**   3
   **D**   4

---

**14** What is another name for $6 + (3 \times 2)$?

   **A**   $(6 + 3) \times 2$
   **B**   $(6 \times 3) + 2$
   **C**   $(3 \times 6) + 2$
   **D**   $6 + (2 \times 3)$

---

**15** Round and then estimate how much is $79 \times 99$.

   **A**   7000
   **B**   8000
   **C**   8800
   **D**   7700

---

**16** What numbers should go in the square and the circle to make this problem true?

$$631 \div 6 = \square, \text{R} \bigcirc$$

   **A**   $\square = 101, \bigcirc = 5$

   **B**   $\square = 100, \bigcirc = 1$

   **C**   $\square = 105, \bigcirc = 5$

   **D**   Not Given

---

**17** Which of these is another way to write $12/16$?

   **A**   $3/4$
   **B**   $2/3$
   **C**   $2/4$
   **D**   $1/4$

---

**18** What is the least common denominator of $1/3$, $1/4$, and $1/12$?

   **A**   3
   **B**   12
   **C**   6
   **D**   24

GO

Cut along dashed line.

**19** Which group shows the fractions ordered from least to greatest?

**A** 1/2, 1/3, 1/4, 1/5

**B** 2/4, 2/3, 2/5, 2/7

**C** 1/5, 2/4, 3/6, 1/4

**D** 1/5, 1/4, 1/3, 1/2

**20** Which of these is a prime number?

**A** 6

**B** 10

**C** 11

**D** 12

**21** Which of these statements is correct?

**A** All even numbers can be divided evenly by 3.

**B** Adding an even number and an even number will always produce an odd number.

**C** Adding an even number and an odd number will always produce an even number.

**D** All even numbers can be divided evenly by 2.

Cut along dashed line.

STOP

# MATH COMPUTATION

**Directions:** Mark the correct answer for each problem. Choose "not given" if the right answer is not given.

**1** $34 \times 8 =$
- **A** 272
- **B** 264
- **C** 306
- **D** Not Given

**2** $11.92
+ 0.29
- **A** $12.22
- **B** $12.21
- **C** $12.01
- **D** $12.11

**3** $329 - 237 =$
- **A** 91
- **B** 93
- **C** 82
- **D** 92

**4** $425 \div 4 =$
- **A** 106
- **B** 106 R 1
- **C** 105 R 1
- **D** Not Given

**5** $\frac{1}{4}$
$+ \frac{2}{5}$
- **A** $13/10$
- **B** $3/20$
- **C** $13/20$
- **D** Not Given

**6** $2 - 3/7 =$
- **A** $4/7$
- **B** $1 3/7$
- **C** $2 4/7$
- **D** $1 4/7$

**7** 633
$\times 28$
- **A** 16, 624
- **B** 17,724
- **C** 17,742
- **D** 17,842

**8** 4.02
$- .79$
- **A** 3.21
- **B** 3.23
- **C** 4.23
- **D** Not Given

**9** $5000 - 4125 =$
- **A** 825
- **B** 775
- **C** 850
- **D** 875

**10** Rose works at a large dairy farm gathering eggs and packing them into cartons that hold one dozen eggs each. Rose gathers 221 eggs. How many cartons will she need and how many eggs will be left over?
- **A** 18 cartons with 4 eggs left over
- **B** 18 cartons with 5 eggs left over
- **C** 17 cartons with 17 eggs left over
- **D** Not Given

GO →

Cut along dashed line.

**11** Two lines that will never intersect are said to be

    **A**   perpendicular
    **B**   similar
    **C**   parallel
    **D**   congruent

**12** What is the area of a square that has one side that is 5 cm long?

    **A**   $10 \text{ cm}^2$
    **B**   $25 \text{ cm}^2$
    **C**   $20 \text{ cm}^2$
    **D**   Not Given

**13** A rectangular prism is 2 units wide, 4 units long, and 8 units high. What is its volume?

    **A**   32 units
    **B**   14 units
    **C**   48 units
    **D**   64 units

**14** Patrick made the following grades on his math tests so far this semester. What is his average grade so far?

| Math Grades | |
| --- | --- |
| Test 1 | 96 |
| Test 2 | 94 |
| Test 3 | 91 |
| Test 4 | 90 |
| Test 5 | 89 |
| Test 6 | 92 |

    **A**   92
    **B**   90
    **C**   91
    **D**   94

**Directions:** Read the problem and use it to answer questions 15 and 16.

Adelia wants to wallpaper one wall in her room. Her mother has given her permission to find out how much money it would cost to buy the wallpaper. The wall measures 8 feet by 12 feet. A roll can cover up to 50 square feet. A package of the border at $12.50 a package can either be put along the top of the wall without any other wallpaper or it can be used on a wall covered with wallpaper. Adelia would need two packages of the border.

**15** How much would it cost if Adelia put up only a border on the wall?

    **A**   $25.00
    **B**   $8.00
    **C**   $16.00
    **D**   $12.00

**16** How much wallpaper does Adelia need for the wall?

    **A**   1 roll
    **B**   2 rolls
    **C**   3 rolls
    **D**   4 rolls

**17** Ms. Jones gave a test to her World History class. The grades were: 64, 70, 72, 80, 80, 80, 88, 90

What grade represented the mode for the class?

    **A**   64
    **B**   95
    **C**   78
    **D**   80

**18** Using the same grades as in question 14, what grade represented the mean for the class?

    **A**   64
    **B**   95
    **C**   78
    **D**   80

Cut along dashed line.

**19** Tiffany sells educational toys. She often sets up a booth at school carnivals. She wants to have enough of her popular toys to sell at the next carnival, so she studies her sales from the last three events.

Carnival A: 25 Nature Kits and 15 Fraction Pies

Carnival B: 20 Nature Kits and 19 Fraction Pies

Carnival C: 24 Nature Kits and 20 Fraction Pies

What should Tiffany order to be sure she doesn't run out of best-sellers?

**A**   20 Nature Kits and 20 Fraction Pies
**B**   25 Nature Kits and 20 Fraction Pies
**C**   25 Nature Kits and 15 Fraction Pies
**D**   20 Nature Kits and 15 Fraction Pies

# Answer Key for Sample Practice Test

## Vocabulary

| | |
|---|---|
| 1 | B |
| 2 | D |
| 3 | D |
| 4 | C |
| 5 | A |
| 6 | C |
| 7 | A |
| 8 | D |
| 9 | B |
| 10 | C |
| 11 | A |
| 12 | D |
| 13 | B |
| 14 | C |

## Reading Comprehension

| | |
|---|---|
| 1 | C |
| 2 | D |
| 3 | A |
| 4 | C |
| 5 | C |
| 6 | B |
| 7 | A |
| 8 | D |
| 9 | C |
| 10 | D |
| 11 | B |
| 12 | B |
| 13 | A |
| 14 | D |

## Language Mechanics

| | |
|---|---|
| 1 | B |
| 2 | A |
| 3 | C |
| 4 | D |
| 5 | C |
| 6 | A |
| 7 | B |
| 8 | D |
| 9 | A |
| 10 | C |
| 11 | A |
| 12 | D |

## Language Expression

| | |
|---|---|
| 1 | B |
| 2 | D |
| 3 | A |
| 4 | C |
| 5 | B |
| 6 | C |
| 7 | D |
| 8 | A |
| 9 | D |
| 10 | B |
| 11 | C |
| 12 | B |
| 13 | D |
| 14 | C |
| 15 | D |
| 16 | A |

## Spelling

| | |
|---|---|
| 1 | A |
| 2 | B |
| 3 | D |
| 4 | C |
| 5 | B |
| 6 | B |
| 7 | A |
| 8 | B |

## Study Skills

| | |
|---|---|
| 1 | A |
| 2 | D |
| 3 | C |
| 4 | B |
| 5 | C |
| 6 | A |
| 7 | D |
| 8 | D |
| 9 | B |
| 10 | C |
| 11 | A |
| 12 | B |

## Math Concepts

| | |
|---|---|
| 1 | D |
| 2 | D |
| 3 | C |
| 4 | C |
| 5 | B |
| 6 | A |
| 7 | C |
| 8 | A |

| | |
|---|---|
| 9 | B |
| 10 | B |
| 11 | A |
| 12 | C |
| 13 | D |
| 14 | D |
| 15 | B |
| 16 | D |
| 17 | A |
| 18 | B |
| 19 | D |
| 20 | C |
| 21 | D |

## Math Computation

| | |
|---|---|
| 1 | A |
| 2 | B |
| 3 | D |
| 4 | B |
| 5 | C |
| 6 | D |
| 7 | B |
| 8 | B |
| 9 | D |
| 10 | B |
| 11 | C |
| 12 | B |
| 13 | D |
| 14 | A |
| 15 | A |
| 16 | B |
| 17 | D |
| 18 | C |
| 19 | B |